bright
baby

bright
baby

Dr. Richard C. Woolfson

BARRON'S

Contents

Introduction **6**

Summary of Development **12**

- Nature or Nurture 14 • Birth Order and Personality 16
- Sibling Rivalry **18** • Gender Differences **20** • Grandparents **22**
- Your Baby's Nonverbal Communication **24** • Crying **26**
- Feeding and Weaning **28** • Sleeping Patterns **30**
- Discipline **32** • Confidence **34** • Special Needs **36**

Development Charts **38**

- From Birth to 3 Months **38** • From 4 to 6 Months **40**
- From 7 to 9 Months **42** • From 10 to 12 Months **44**
- From 13 to 15 Months **46**

Movement **48**

- The Development of Movement **50** • Charts **52–5**
- Stimulating Movement – Activities **56–65**

Hand–Eye Coordination **66**

- The Importance of Hand–Eye Coordination **68** • Charts **70–3**
- Stimulating Hand–Eye Coordination – Activities **74–83**

Language   **84**

• The Development of Language **86** • Charts **88–91**
• Stimulating Language – Activities **92–101**

Learning   **102**

• The Development of Learning Skills **104** • Charts **106–9**
• Stimulating Learning – Activities **110–19**

Social and Emotional Development   **120**

• Social and Emotional Development: Birth to 15 Months **122**
• Charts **124–7** • Stimulating Social and Emotional
Development – Activities **128–37**

Index of Age Groups   **138**

General Index   **139**

Acknowledgments   **144**

The Importance of Stimulation

Your child's first year is an amazing time for him and for you, and provides the foundation on which all his subsequent development is built. At birth, he arrives into this world with an inquiring mind, ready to explore and discover – and during the next year, his skills and abilities develop further, extending all the time. Your young baby is an active, dynamic learner who has an innate need to learn, and you will see this every day as his curiosity seems never-ending. Yet you can help this process along by providing him with love, care, and stimulation so that he becomes a bright baby.

Your Active Learner

Right from birth, your baby demonstrates his desire to learn. He wants to make sense of the world around him, and he does everything he can to reach out and explore. Of course, in the initial weeks of life he has little control of his hand, arm, leg, and body movements, but that doesn't stop him from actively building his knowledge.

For instance, he stares closely at any person or object that comes close to him, he tastes anything that is put into his mouth, and he grabs hold of a small object that is put into his hand. He is an active learner who uses every skill he has to extend his

Left: At just a few days old, babies can fix their gaze on an object brought into their range of vision.

understanding, whether he is 1 week old or 1 year old.

The fact that your baby has an inborn desire to explore and discover is great, because it means he is predisposed to improve and deliberately seeks out new challenges and learning opportunities. For example, when left alone in his crib your month-

old baby will perhaps pull the crib blanket up to his face so that he can study it closely, feel it, and even chew it. At the age of 6 months, he will do his best to pull his body along the floor to reach any object that attracts his attention. And at around 1 year, he will toddle about the house, exploring areas that he couldn't reach previously.

Below: This little girl's fascination with pouring water shows how easy it is to make everyday events like bathtime stimulating for your baby.

You'll love watching him in these self-motivated learning situations as you take pride in his endless enthusiasm and ever-increasing skills. Yet that doesn't mean that as a parent you should sit back and leave it all to chance. On the contrary, if this is what he can achieve on his own, imagine what he could achieve with your help!

The Importance of Stimulation
Stimulation from you – using the activities and ideas suggested throughout this book – will provide your baby's development with a further boost. Your stimulation doesn't replace his natural drive to become a bright baby; rather it enhances and extends it. Here are some of the many benefits for your baby when you carry out activities to stimulate him:

• **personal attention.** The very fact that you spend time with him in a caring, loving atmosphere is good for him. Activities bring you closer to each other and your baby thrives on this attention. And he's more likely to learn when he is relaxed and comfortable than when he is fed up and feeling lonely.

• **within his reach.** While your baby spontaneously plays with anything he lays his hands on, his restricted movement and hand–eye coordination mean that most objects are beyond his reach. By bringing toys and other activities to your baby, you immediately overcome this natural limitation on his learning.

Above: Eye contact and talking to your baby are very important – changing time provides a good opportunity.

• **extend his skills.** Through involvement with your baby, you can teach him new ways of playing with familiar toys. The moment you show him that, for instance, a rattle makes a noise when it is moved, he has learned something new and is stimulated to play with this toy in a way that he couldn't before.

Below: Your encouragement, enthusiasm, and one-to-one attention are key contributors to your child's development.

◆◆◆◆ Top·Tips ◆◆◆◆

1. Remember that he is an active learner. It's easy to forget that your baby learns all the time, even when you are not doing anything in particular to stimulate him. He actively learns every single day just from being with you.

2. Look on stimulation as a partnership. He may only be a young baby but he is not passive. Expect your baby to react, to show that he has connected with the toy or game, before moving on to another activity.

3. Offer activities appropriately. You may feel tempted to give your baby toys suitable for an older child because you think this will boost his progress. But this could have the opposite effect, so offer activities at his level.

4. Laugh with him. Although stimulation is a serious business, it must be enjoyable for you and your baby or you'll both lose interest. Smile at him and laugh with him whenever possible.

5. Be proud of your bright baby. Delight in every new skill he acquires, in every new achievement he makes. Love him for his uniqueness, not for how well he compares with other babies his age.

Using this Book

You will be able to provide a more effective level of stimulation when you understand the process of development more fully. And by identifying the key areas of growth during this first year you can target your baby's stimulation in specific directions. For instance, you might decide to improve her language skills, or her hand–eye control, but each area of development interacts so that progress in one area influences progress in another. A holistic approach to stimulating your baby is the most powerful approach, rather than targeting each dimension individually. The ideas and suggestions in this book give you an all-around strategy for stimulating your bright baby.

How to Use this Book

There are many ways to categorize infant development. This book focuses on five main dimensions, and there is an entire chapter devoted to each of the following, although they all interact with one another:

• **movement.** This is your baby's ability to move her arms, legs, and body in a coordinated and purposeful way. At birth, her physical movement is extremely limited and she remains more or less in the same spot unless you move her yourself. By the age of 15 months, she can walk independently and go wherever she wants, even up and down stairs.

• **hand–eye coordination.** When she is newly born, your baby's hand control is minimal and she can't, for instance, reach out and grab a toy that is close to her. She tries hard but she just can't deliberately take hold of a small object. Over the next year, however, her hand–eye coordination extends to the point where she can intentionally put her hands out toward a toy and then pick it up.

• **language.** For at least a couple of months, your baby can't make any recognizable speech sounds – crying is her only verbal way of communicating with you. Slowly and steadily during the next 15 months, she progresses from gurgling sounds

Above: As soon as they can grasp, babies instinctively explore objects with their hands and mouth.

to random vowel and consonant sounds, until she reaches that wonderful stage of saying her first word. And what a magical moment that is.

• **learning.** Your baby is pre-programmed to learn, although she is at a very early stage in the process of understanding. She is not aware of basic concepts such as action–reaction (for instance, when

Left: Every baby will master new skills at different rates, so try not to compare her progress against others and let her set her own pace.

a rattle is moved it makes a noise) or object permanence (for instance, when a ball rolls behind the chair it doesn't disappear altogether). By the start of her second year, she has learned a great deal.

• **social and emotional.** Your baby is such a sensitive individual, totally dependent on you for all her emotional needs. She wants you with her at all times, not just to feed, change, and dress her, but also to make her feel safe and secure. Your baby's emotional attachment to you is vital. Throughout the first 15 months, you will see her confidence improve; she also becomes more sociable.

An Overview

Although these different areas of development are discussed in separate chapters in this book, they overlap. That's why it is important to have an overview of your baby's progress, instead of being concerned with only one dimension of development at a time.

For instance, talking to your baby stimulates her language, and also affects her emotional development because your attention makes her feel loved; putting a toy just outside her reach encourages her to use her hand control, her movement skills, her vision and attention; giving her a small inset-board puzzle increases her understanding, extends her hand control, and also boosts her confidence when she achieves success with it. Every activity given in this book has an impact in several areas and therefore makes a multifaceted contribution to your baby's progress.

Each chapter in this book can be read on its own or in conjunction with any other. Feel free to take one activity at random or to use it as part of your planned program of stimulation for your baby. Remember that every single stimulating activity or game played with your child adds something positive to her overall progress.

❖❖❖❖ Top·Tips ❖❖❖❖

1. Understand development. You'll be able to choose activities from this book more appropriately when you have a broad understanding of your child's development. The first half of the book takes an overarching perspective.

2. Pick 'n' mix. You and your baby will have much more fun together with a varied program of stimulation, involving activities that cover as many different areas of development as possible. Avoid focusing on one area exclusively at a time.

3. Know your baby. You know your baby best of all and are aware of her own rate of progress. Use this knowledge to select activities that are suitable for her level, which may not necessarily be ones designated as suitable for her age.

4. Adapt as required. The suggestions given are exactly that: suggestions, not rigid advice. Have the confidence to adapt any of them to suit your baby, the play equipment available, and her specific level of development.

5. Use it as a guide, not an instruction manual. The suggestions in this book should not be carried out slavishly in rote fashion. Try to have a flexible, relaxed approach.

Your Attitude

Your attitude toward your baby's progress significantly affects your relationship with him and the level of stimulation you offer. It's essential to strike a balance between understimulation and overstimulation – in most instances, a baby does not thrive best in extremes. If you take a less involved approach, you could find he is understimulated, causing him to be restless and bored, and that's certainly not helpful for his development; yet if you are too zealous, you could make him overstimulated and miserable, causing him to be tired and irritable. The challenge facing you is to match the level of stimulation to his needs and abilities so that his motivation is high.

Getting the Right Balance

Try to keep a balanced attitude when it comes to stimulating your baby. Either too much or too little can have a detrimental effect. Of course you want the best for your growing baby so that he is bright, lively, and alert. Every parent wants that. But don't fall into the trap of thinking that more of the same necessarily means better. If you think you are pushing your baby too hard – because you see some of the signs mentioned on page 11 – then step back and rethink the program of activities that you provide for him. The same applies if you are worried that he doesn't receive enough stimulation.

The best way to know that you've achieved a healthy balance is to watch your baby. If he is motivated, enjoys his daily toys and games, has a sparkling facial expression, and reacts positively to you when you play with him, you can be pretty sure that you've got his stimulation just right.

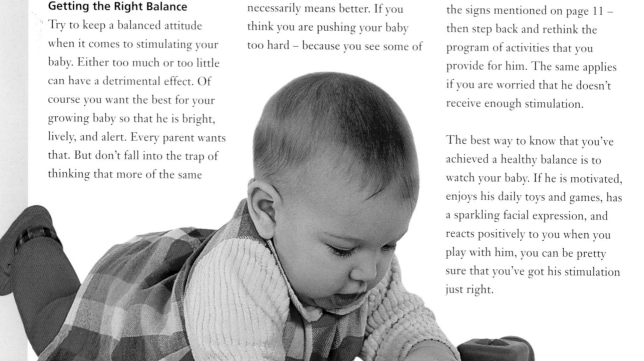

Above: Happily absorbed in her toys, this 7-month-old benefits from some time spent playing by herself.

Five Signs that Your Baby Is Understimulated

If your baby is understimulated, he may have the following characteristics:

1. lack of drive. Lack of stimulation reduces his motivation and general level of activity. He gets so used to having nothing to do that he eventually becomes comfortable with just lying in his crib. He prefers inactivity.

2. passivity. A baby who lacks stimulation soon becomes passive, even when activities and toys are brought to him. Although he might glance at objects that attract attention, he is not prepared to become actively involved.

3. easily upset. He prefers a quiet atmosphere, rather than one full of hustle and bustle. As a result he becomes nervous and agitated when events intrude on his life. He will burst out crying, for instance, if someone tries to play with him.

4. lack of expression. His general lethargy shows in other ways, too. In particular, his facial expressions are less communicative, his smiles are less lively, his eyes are less sparkling. His body movements generally are less dynamic.

5. uncomplaining. Most babies cry occasionally – that's how they let other people know they are unhappy. An understimulated baby cries less frequently because he reacts less to his own discomfort. He settles for less.

Five Signs that Your Baby Is Overstimulated

If your baby is overstimulated, he may have the following characteristics:

1. irritability. In the same way that you start to feel grumpy when too much noise and activity goes on around you, so does your young baby. He doesn't like to be bombarded with stimulating activities every moment of the day.

2. weak concentration. A baby has fluctuating concentration at the best of times. Overstimulation reduces his concentration further still, and you'll find he flits from one toy to the next every few seconds.

Above: Your understanding of your child's personality will help you judge how much and what kind of stimulation he needs.

3. tiredness. Eventually a feeling of weariness sets in. You suddenly find that your infant doesn't reach out for the latest toy you brought home for him. Instead, he just stares at it – he's had enough stimulation for the time being.

4. unsettled. Too much stimulation reduces your baby's need to think for himself; he doesn't have to bother making his own amusement or learning experiences. As a result, he is unsettled until you provide the next episode of stimulation.

5. inability to sleep. Your baby can sleep only when he is relaxed and calm. Overstimulation keeps him too active as bedtime approaches, and he experiences difficulty switching off. His sleeping pattern becomes disrupted.

✦✦✦✦ Top Tips ✦✦✦✦

1. Don't force yourself to play with your baby. If you have had a long, hard day with him and feel too tired to play anymore, then stop. Almost certainly he's as tired as you and would prefer a rest, too.

2. Allow him free play. He needs to have times during the day when he explores, plays, and discovers by himself, without any involvement or direction from you. Make sure he has free-play opportunities each day.

3. Watch the way he plays with toys. If he plays with the same toy every day and his play is repetitive and lacking adventure, it's time to get more involved in order to extend his play skills.

4. Join in without dominating. When stimulating your baby, remember that there is a difference between playing with him and taking over altogether. Offer new ideas but let him be the one who plays with the toys, not you.

5. Keep it fun. Both you and your baby should enjoy your involvement with each other. If the fun goes out of play – for either you or your baby – there may be either too little or too much stimulation.

Summary of

Development

Nature or Nurture

Your position regarding the nature/nurture debate affects your interactions with your baby. If you believe in the "nature" argument, then you'll assume that her inborn characteristics, learning abilities, and personality determine what sort of person she becomes, and that your own individual input as a parent does not have much to do with it. If you believe in the "nurture" argument, however, you'll assume that her development is dependent entirely on the way you raise her and the level of stimulation she experiences during her childhood. You might take a middle-of-the-road approach, recognizing the importance of both your baby's innate talents and also the environment in which she is raised.

Each Side

The nature/nurture debate is also known as the heredity/environment debate. The term "nature" applies to all the characteristics and qualities that a child has at birth, even though they are not entirely obvious at this early stage. Many physical characteristics are inherited from parents and predetermine certain aspects of a child's development. For instance, your baby's genetic structure determines what color her eyes and hair will be, what her typical height will be, and even her natural body weight.

The "nature" argument runs along the line that says because many physical qualities are inherited, it stands to reason that many psychological characteristics are also inherited. That's why, for instance, children often have the same personality and mannerisms as their parents. If physical traits can be inherited at conception and be present at birth, perhaps the whole pattern of a child's development is also inherited in the same way.

In contrast, the term "nurture" suggests that many characteristics are influenced by the child's environment, particularly by the way she is brought up within the family. For instance, bright parents make their baby's stimulation a priority and therefore tend to have bright children, and sensitive parents teach their children to behave in a similar caring way when mixing with others. Some take this argument further, claiming that no personal characteristics whatsoever are inherited and that every child is born a *tabula rasa* (blank slate) waiting for her development to be written by experience.

Left: Your baby will display his own unique character from birth, even down to how he prefers to be carried.

Interaction

Few child development professionals adopt either extreme approach. Instead, it is widely recognized that although every child has potential based on her genetic structure at birth, the true influence on her development is the interaction that takes place between her inherited abilities and the environment in which she is

Left: Whatever her inherited traits, loving parental attention will increase a baby's sense of enjoyment and security.

brought up. The nature/nurture debate nowadays is not an either/or discussion but centers around the relative contribution that each influence makes to your baby's growth and progress. There is evidence to support both sides.

Studies of twins who were separated and raised by different families as a result of their adoption at birth have found striking similarities between the personality and abilities of each twin, despite their individual upbringing. In addition, similarities are found between adopted children and their birth parents, even though the children were raised by others. This type of scientific data adds considerable weight to the inherited view of child development.

Yet there are many instances in which even those physical characteristics that are *undoubtedly* inherited can be directly influenced by the environment. To take

Right: The way you stimulate and encourage your baby during the first 15 months really does matter.

height as an example, a child may have the genetic potential to grow to a certain height but she is unlikely to achieve that if she is undernourished during the preschool years. Other factors such as health, poverty, and family values have a similar effect. Evidence shows that children who are raised in a family where violence is the norm are more aggressive in their interactions with peers.

Your baby's development is a combination of all these factors and the way they interact at each point in her life. Parenting, therefore, is not about stepping back while passively waiting for the genetic plan to unfold. What you do with your growing baby makes a real difference to her long-term development.

❖❖❖ Top·Tips ❖❖❖

1. Take a hands-on approach. Nobody can quantify exactly what effect you have on your baby, but common sense and everyday experience tell you that she is affected greatly by the way you behave toward her.

2. Have reasonable expectations. Although you can affect your baby's progress, you are unlikely to see instant changes in her development. Expect her to progress in small, steady steps and you won't be disappointed.

3. Treat her individually. Your baby may have the same parents and the same family environment as her siblings, but she reacts to these in her own unique way. Development is not entirely predictable, varying from child to child.

4. Take pleasure from her achievements. Whether arising from "nature" or "nurture," savor all of your baby's increased abilities and skills. This makes her feel good about herself and motivates her to continue to progress.

5. Stimulate your baby anyway. The inability of professionals to specify the precise effect you can have on your baby's development shouldn't discourage you from implementing the activities suggested in this book. Do it anyway.

Birth Order and Personality

There is a link between your baby's birth order and his subsequent development. In other words, his progress during childhood is to some extent affected by his position within the family (that is, for instance, whether he is your firstborn, your middle child, an only child, or your youngest). Evidence from research confirms that some characteristics – including temperament, learning skills, problem-solving ability, social skills, and confidence – are associated with each of the major birth positions. Remember, however, that birth order is only one of the many influences on your baby's development, and that its effect can be offset by the way you raise him.

Above: Older children often dominate younger brothers and sisters, and at times you may need to intervene.

Typical Characteristics

Here are some key findings from psychological research:

• **firstborn babies tend to be more intelligent than their siblings, and they tend to think clearly and rationally.** They are likely to be the most successful in life, compared with their siblings.

• **second children frequently are less concerned with following rules.** They prefer to go against the grain and to challenge conventional

thinking. Your second-born baby may push your rules to the limits.

• **youngest children are the most able of all the children in the family to cope with the stresses and strains of everyday life.** Your youngest child is likely to be confident, and to be able to handle problems on his own without seeking help.

• **middle children are usually the most even-tempered, and are adept at solving disputes peacefully.** Your middle child is also likely to be protective

Right: Younger brothers and sisters learn a great deal from watching, copying, and playing with their older siblings.

toward his older and younger siblings. She may occasionally feel left out of things.

• **only children typically mix well with adults.** The chances are, though, that your only child is self-sufficient, and when he mixes with others he shows good leadership qualities.

How Birth Order Operates

When you think about it for a moment, you'll have no difficulty understanding why these various effects of birth order occur. Take your firstborn baby, for example. He has you all to himself for the first part of his life – he may be 2 years or older before the next one arrives – and this means you spend all your child-focused time with him. The effort you put into stimulating his development doesn't have to be shared with any other child. With that level of attention from you, it's hardly surprising that he's so bright, alert, and highly motivated.

And the fact that later-born children like to bend the rules and seek the outrageous rather than the traditional is probably owing to the fact that they want to be different from their older brother or sister. Your second-born child wants to carve his own destiny; he doesn't want to be in the shadow of his high-achieving older sister, and the best way to avoid that trap, as far as

Below: It is important to share one-to-one attention fairly between your children, but there are also plenty of opportunities for everyone to join in the fun.

he is concerned, is to follow a different path altogether.

The reason youngest children tend to be the most independent is largely because of necessity. There's nothing like living with the prospect of being always at the back of the family line to sharpen your youngest child's survival skills!

Taking Control

Try to understand how birth order could mold your child's development, because that will help you to ensure that he doesn't become unduly affected by this potential influence. Look at your child's life from his point of view and imagine what it must be like to have that particular family position.

Then do what you can to make sure that birth order doesn't have a disproportionate effect on his life. For example, make a specific point of spending time stimulating your second child even though you now have two to look after; don't always assume that your older child should be responsible for his younger siblings when they play together; let your younger child sometimes be the one to choose the television program the family watches.

Sibling Rivalry

The moment you have your second child – in fact, the moment your firstborn baby realizes she has a little brother or sister on the way – you need to consider the possibility of sibling rivalry. Jealousy between children in the same family is so common that most psychologists regard it as normal, and it arises because each of your children has to compete for her own share of parental time and attention. The extent to which sibling rivalry occurs depends on many factors, including the age gap between your children, the techniques you use to help them resolve conflicts, and the way in which you relate to them.

About Sibling Rivalry

Jealousy of brothers and sisters can show in a variety of ways. Your 2-year-old, for example, could become moody and withdrawn around the time her younger sister is born, or your 4-year-old might complain that her 2-year-old brother constantly takes her toys without asking. But sibling rivalry isn't confined just to the firstborn child. There is evidence from psychological research that second-born and third-born children can resent a new baby, even though they are already used to living with others in the family. The youngest child can also be jealous of her older siblings; your 15-month-old toddler might burst into tears when she sees you cuddling her older sister because she wants all your love for herself.

You are most likely to experience sibling rivalry with your children when your youngest is around the age of 3 or 4 years – it's at this age that she makes a serious effort to assert herself, and a sibling is often

seen as a threat at that point in time. When your child is around 2 years old, she will probably express her jealousy by hitting her sibling rather than by speaking to her. Don't be surprised, however, at the individual differences between your children when it comes to the subject of sibling rivalry; one

might be very concerned about everything her brother does, whereas another might not show any concern at all.

Below: Let your toddler touch her new brother or sister gently. She needs to feel involved in the baby's arrival as much as possible.

The age gap between your children can also have an effect on the intensity of jealousy between them. Research shows, for instance, that sibling rivalry tends to be at its highest when the age gap separating children is between 18 months and 2 years, and it tends to be lowest when the age gap is either much smaller or much larger. When the firstborn child is very young at the birth of the second baby, she will barely notice the new arrival because she is so concerned with herself. When the firstborn is several years older when the second baby arrives she probably won't feel threatened by the presence of a new baby because she is secure in her relationships and has an established daily routine.

When She's Just a Toddler

It's the in-between age gap that causes most problems. The typical toddler likes to have everything her own way and wants the world to revolve around her. She may be upset by a new baby in the family because that younger sibling needs lots of attention, too.

If you are pregnant with your second child while your firstborn is still a young toddler, tell her about the new baby once your pregnancy starts to show, probably around the fourth or fifth month. Explain that the new baby will love her and that you'll love her just as much, too. She needs your reassurance at this time, so answer openly and honestly any questions she has. Let her buy a present for the new baby and make sure that the new baby has a present for her at their first meeting (a gift that you packed in your hospital bag before you went in).

Remember that your firstborn just needs to feel loved and valued, especially when the new baby is the focus of attention. Despite the hectic routine of caring for a second baby at the same time as looking after a toddler, try to find time to be on your own with your firstborn every day.

Below: Encourage your children to play together and cooperate with each other, including during their daily routine.

✦✦✦✦ Top · Tips ✦✦✦✦

1. Avoid comparing one child another. Few things are more likely to cause antagonism and resentment of siblings than pointing out to one child that her older brother is, for instance, more clever, more responsible, or more helpful.

2. Encourage your children to cooperate with each other. Suggest that they play with their toys together sometimes or that they tidy up together. Watch them as they do this so that you can teach them how to cooperate.

3. Help them resolve disagreements. Instead of getting angry at their constant bickering, sit your children down and encourage them to discuss their disagreements. That's a lot better than letting them fight their way to a solution.

4. Treat your children individually. This does not mean that you should relate to each of them the exact same way, but it does mean you should try to meet their individual needs as they arise.

5. Praise them when they do play together. If your children get along well with each other, let them know that you are pleased with their behavior. Tell them that the atmosphere is a lot more pleasant when they don't bicker.

Gender Differences

The differences between boys and girls are not just biological; there are significant psychological differences, too. However, people often hold mistaken stereotyped views on gender. For instance, some claim that boy babies cry more than girl babies; in reality, they cry for equal amounts of time, but the deeper voice tones of boys might make it seem as though they cry for longer. And some claim that girl babies are more fragile than boy babies, yet female embryos are stronger than male embryos, and are less susceptible to miscarriage. It's important to sort out fact from fiction, because your expectations of boys and girls affect your baby's development.

Facts About Gender

Here are some facts about gender differences up to the age of 15 months:

• **a baby boy is typically more adventurous than a baby girl; he is more likely to take risks.** Yet there is evidence that parents tacitly accept this type of behavior from boys but not from girls, and so tend to inadvertently encourage such differences.

• **boys tend to have more problems with their development than girls, and girls usually learn to speak their first word before boys.**

Girls also tend to have better hand–eye coordination during the first year.

• **parents react differently to baby boys and baby girls.** For example, they are more likely to tolerate aggressive behavior from a boy than from a girl. Aggression is discouraged immediately when shown by a baby girl.

Below: This little boy seems more outgoing than does the little girl in his willingness to reach out to her.

Your baby's awareness of gender differences emerges very early on. At the age of only 3 months, he can tell the difference between a woman's face and a man's face. For instance, if he is shown dozens of photographs of women's faces he will gradually lose interest and let his attention wander, but the moment he sees a photograph of a man,

his concentration will suddenly pick up again.

Within a few months his ability to recognize gender extends not just to faces but also to voices. Researchers showed babies a series of pictures of men and women, each one accompanied by either a man's voice or a woman's voice. When the gender of the voice matched the gender of the photograph, the babies would look at the picture for longer than when there was a mismatch. By 6 months, therefore, your baby differentiates between men and women just by voice tones.

By 1 year he probably shows a preference for playing with boys rather than girls when he finds himself in mixed company. A research study found that 1-year-old infants still managed to play with children of the same gender as themselves, even when they all wore unisex clothing.

The Source of Gender

One explanation of gender differences rests on the scientific fact that there are biological differences between boys and girls. For example, during pregnancy and at birth, boys have a higher level of testosterone, which is linked to aggression and high activity. And there are those who claim that since women are physically equipped to bear children and men are not, they must have a biological instinct to be caring and domestic; that's why, continue these theorists, girls enjoy playing with dolls whereas boys prefer more adventurous activities.

The other main explanation of gender differences rests on the assumption that these differences are learned. For instance, few parents describe their new baby boy as "pretty" and buy him pink clothes, or describe their new baby girl as "handsome" and buy her blue clothes. Through this process, these theorists claim, gender differences are reinforced by the view on gender differences that parents already hold.

There is no clear answer to this debate on the origins of gender differences. It stands to reason that there is a biological component to gender differences, but it also makes sense to accept that the influence of parents must also play a part. These separate factors interact to create your baby's views on gender.

Left: If parents don't discourage it, little boys will enjoy playing with dolls and teddy bears just as little girls will enjoy toy trains.

❖❖❖❖ Top·Tips ❖❖❖❖

1. Be self-aware. Think about your own attitudes about boys and girls. Be prepared to give as much encouragement to your baby girl when she starts to explore as you would to your baby boy.

2. Give him a wide range of toys. There is no point in keeping soft toys and dolls away from your baby boy, and surrounding your baby girl with them. Don't worry if he shows interest in toys you normally associate with girls.

3. Show affection to your baby, whether a boy or a girl. Your baby boy likes to be loved and cuddled by you just as much as your baby girl. No matter what his individual characteristics, he wants your attention and plenty of hugs.

4. Have confidence in your parenting ability. Rely on your instincts, and don't be concerned about what others tell you about the way boys and girls should behave. There is no "should" about it – it is entirely up to you.

5. Set a good example. Your baby's views on gender are also influenced by your attitudes and behavior. If, for instance, only women change him and play with him, then he will grow up thinking this is the sole province of women.

Grandparents

Your baby's grandparents can play such an important and special role in her life. They'll probably be delighted to have the opportunity to devote their love, attention, and resources to her, savoring any chance at all to spend time with their grandchild. This relationship adds to your baby's development. And her grandparents can also play a big part in your own life as a parent. They have experience with raising children themselves, and they will be eager to share this with you in order to help you manage your baby. Of course there is the danger that grandparents can become too dominant, but this can usually be dealt with effectively using sensitive management.

Getting Involved

The traditional stereotype of grandparents portrays them as over-indulgent, willing to spoil their beloved grandchild whenever they can. Psychological research, however, shows that the true picture is more complex. Nowadays, grandparents tend to be younger than previously (in their forties or early fifties) and are likely to be fit, active, and in full-time employment themselves. They are, therefore, less likely to have as much free time to spend with their grandchild. On the other hand, more children than ever before live with their grandparents (not always

Right: Grandparents are often in a position to give a child concentrated love and attention away from the stresses of everyday family life.

with their parents, too), and in these instances the grandparents are the ones who look after the child.

Your baby loves it when your parents come to visit – her excitement at their arrival is clearly visible. However, she will form a stronger emotional attachment to her grandparents when she also spends time alone with them,

when you are not there. It's not so much that grandparents are inhibited by their own children's presence, just that their grandchild is more likely to give them all her attention. They need to spend time together to cement this special connection.

Grandparenting Styles

Not all grandparents relate to their grandchild in the

same way. Psychologists have identified a number of "grandparenting styles," each describing a different way that grandparents get involved in family life:

• **traditional.** These grandparents like to visit their grandchild regularly, and accept any opportunity to baby-sit her. Yet

they try not to dominate in case their own child accuses them of trying to interfere in the way the baby is raised.

• **playful.** These grandparents want to be more involved and will play with their grandchild and take her on outings with them whenever possible. They want a warm, caring relationship with her, one that is based on mutual love.

• **authoritarian.** These grandparents see themselves as the head of the family and think that their children should look up to them in all matters, especially when it comes to the way grandchildren should be raised. They have very fixed ideas.

• **remote.** Changes in society mean that in many instances the grandparents live far away from the grandchildren, perhaps on the opposite side of the city or in a different city altogether. They have few chances to be with their grandchild.

Whatever style your baby's grandparents adopt, remember that a positive relationship between your baby and them – and between you and them – will be in her best interest. Your baby's relationship with you won't be threatened by her strong emotional connection with them; on the contrary, the happier she is, the easier she'll relate to

everyone in her life. She can love you dearly and love them at the same time.

That's why it is best to resolve any points of tension between you and your baby's grandparents as soon as they arise. In families, little misunderstandings can easily grow into huge disagreements if they are not addressed properly, and before you know it, you and your baby's grandparents have fallen out with each other. So if you find that you are in disagreement with them – perhaps because they did something with your baby when you had asked them not to – be candid and direct with them, expressing your feelings openly but calmly and tactfully. Honest communication is the best way to reduce tension.

Right: Grandparents can make valuable practical contributions in helping to care for their grandchildren.

✦✦✦✦ Top·Tips ✦✦✦✦

1. Make them welcome in your home. Grandparents won't visit where they are not welcome; they don't want to be thought of as pushy or intrusive. Make your invitations to them very clear so that they know you want them to call.

2. Let them baby-sit your baby. You may not agree with all their views on raising children, but using them as baby-sitters is good for them, for you, and for your baby. They are parents themselves, so you know that she is safe with them.

3. Listen to their advice. Of course you are the parent and they are the grandparents, and decisions about the way your baby is cared for rest with you. Yet there is no harm in at least listening to the grandparents' comments.

4. Offer suggestions for play. It's probably a long time since they last played with a baby, and at first they might not be sure what to do. Suggest toys and activities for them to play with her. Their confidence will quickly build.

5. Share happy moments with them. They'll be delighted to hear of every new achievement that your baby makes, every new stage that she reaches. And their pleasure adds to your own excitement. Keep them closely informed.

Your Baby's Nonverbal Communication

Until your baby develops meaningful spoken language (usually by the end of the first year), he relies on nonverbal communication to express his feelings and ideas to you. Aside from crying as a means of communication, your baby uses body language such as facial expressions, and arm and leg movements. The more you can understand his body language at this stage, the closer the emotional connection between you and your baby. In addition to tuning in to his preverbal communication, you can do a lot to encourage him to use nonverbal communication more effectively.

Dimensions of Your Baby's Nonverbal Communication

The main features of body language during the first 15 months are

• **crying.** This is your baby's instinctive way of letting you know that he is unhappy. Initially he cries only when he is hungry or in pain, but his cries gradually become more varied and expressive as the months pass by.

• **facial expression.** Your baby can convey a whole range of emotions simply by changing the expression on his face. Just by looking at his appearance, you can tell when he is, for instance, happy, sad, contented, uncomfortable, tired, afraid, hurting, or angry.

• **arm and hand movements.** Within a few months, your baby starts to use his hands to reach out for things that he wants, and also to push objects or people away. This is a clear expression of his desires, and you have no difficulty understanding him.

• **leg and feet movements.** When he is lying in his crib as a young

baby, vigorous leg movements could indicate he is happy and excited, or they could mean he is upset and in pain. When more mobile, he walks away from something he dislikes.

• **body movements.** You know that your baby is not settled if he

Above: At 5 months old this little girl's startled look reveals exactly how she is feeling.

wriggles about in his crib. Instinctively you ask him, "What's wrong?" because his sporadic body movements have told you he is not happy or he is uncomfortable.

• **physical contact.** Snuggling up to you for a warm, cozy cuddle tells you immediately that your baby is at ease with you and likes your company. He tells you exactly the opposite when he struggles furiously in your arms.

The more you respond to your baby's body language the more he sees the purpose in communication – and that's good for his language development, too. So try to tune in to the meaning of his nonverbal communication. You will find that very soon you can tell what he wants to say. And when you find that you have interpreted his body language accurately – for instance, he stopped crying once you changed his diaper – this gives you increased confidence in your own ability to respond to your baby's needs. It also increases his trust in you as a caring, loving parent.

Bear in mind that the same gesture can have a different meaning in different contexts. For example, throwing a toy onto the floor could indicate excitement, anger, or even plain boredom. So look for clusters of gestures, those that involve a

•••• Top•Tips ••••

1. Watch him. The best way to become familiar with your baby's body language is to observe him in different situations. You will gradually learn the many ways in which he communicates to you nonverbally.

2. Do something practical. If you think he is trying to say something to you that requires some action (for example, he is excited because he sees you and wants a cuddle), carry out that action. This reinforces his desire to communicate.

3. Imitate his actions. If you are not sure what his body language is saying to you, you might be able to get a better understanding by copying his gestures yourself – ask yourself what it feels like when making these movements.

4. Tell your baby your interpretation. Say to him, for instance, "I can see you are telling me that you want something to eat." This helps him learn that there is a connection between nonverbal communication and spoken language.

5. Discuss with others. You will find it helpful to talk to other people about your baby's body language, assuming they know him well. You can match your opinion with theirs to judge the accuracy of your interpretation.

combination of facial expression, arm and leg movements, and body movements. You'll get a more accurate picture of his communication when you interpret a cluster of body language rather than a specific gesture on its own.

Talking

Although your young baby is at a preverbal stage and therefore uses body language to connect with you, you should still talk to him using spoken language. This boosts his nonverbal communication in a number of ways. First, it lets him see that you are able to communicate with him and he tries harder to respond to what you say.

Above: The little girl's smile and hand movement (left) show her excitement at something she has seen. The little boy's expression and gesture tell us that he has bumped his head, though not very badly!

Secondly, he studies your facial expression very closely while you talk to him, so he learns about nonverbal features such as eyes, forehead, mouth, and voice tone. Your baby uses your body language as a model to copy himself.

Thirdly, talking to your baby eases his frustrations, making him feel he is understood, and that calm emotional state encourages him to be more communicative.

Crying

All babies cry from time to time, though some cry more than others. Crying is your baby's way of telling you that she is troubled about something; for instance, she could be uncomfortable, in pain, cold, hungry, tired, bored, or thirsty. It is her natural mode of communication before she can use spoken language. At first all her cries sound the same, but you will steadily get to know what each type of cry means. Your baby cries most frequently during the first 3 months, and then her crying trails off. Research has also found that many babies cry without any explicit source of discomfort.

What to Do

When your young baby cries, always check out the obvious possibilities first. Perhaps she needs to eat, or maybe she is too cold. Also consider the possibility that she simply wants attention, or that she doesn't feel well. Once you have ruled out these options, give her a big reassuring cuddle – that might not stop her crying immediately but it will help. The warmth of loving physical contact and the vibrations of your beating heart reassure your sobbing baby. You'll feel happier, too, knowing that you are holding her close to you.

Although you may become agitated by her tears, don't let persistent crying get you down. Between birth and the age of 3 months, she probably cries for around a total of two hours every single day (although not all at once). After that, the amount of crying she does

Left: Crying is one way a newborn baby has of communicating her needs.

each day is cut by half, though even one hour a day of crying can pull at your nerves. There is absolutely no evidence to support the popular myth that, as babies, boys cry more than girls.

Soothing Techniques

Try the following strategies for settling your crying baby:
• **movement.** The simple act of gently rocking her back and forth in your arms or in her carriage could have a calming effect. Sometimes she will stop crying if you just change her position in the crib.
• **touch.** She may stop if held gently but firmly in a warm bath. Hugging her close to you could have the same effect. If she is really agitated and doesn't want to be lifted, let her lie in her crib while you gently stroke her cheeks and forehead.
• **sounds.** You'll be amazed how your singing soothes her – it's the sound of your voice, your loving tone, and the familiar rhythm of the

words that she concentrates on. Some babies like a steady background noise such as the sound of a washing machine.
• **amusement.** Sometimes your crying baby can be brought out of her tears by the sight of a toy brought close to her. Her interest in the object makes her momentarily forget her distress and so she suddenly stops crying.

Whatever technique you use with your crying baby, use it consistently before changing to something else. It's very easy to panic when you are faced with a baby who cries regularly for no apparent reason, and to try one thing after another. The problem with that methodology is that your baby can't get used to any of the techniques because you didn't use them for long enough. Persist until you are absolutely sure it has no effect on her tears.

To Pick Up or Not to Pick Up

Almost certainly you will be given conflicting advice about comforting a crying baby. One person will tell

Right: By the time your baby is 4 months old you will have a good idea whether his cries mean he is hungry, tired, uncomfortable, or just wants your attention.

you to leave her when she cries (otherwise she will learn to cry to get your attention) whereas another person will tell you to cuddle her every time (otherwise she will feel lonely and neglected). Both of these suggestions are too extreme, however.

❖❖❖❖ Top·Tips ❖❖❖❖

1. Stay calm. The persistent screaming of a baby can make you want to scream yourself. That would only make your baby more agitated and tearful. Make a big effort to keep control of your temper.

2. Get help. If possible, let another person spend time with your crying baby. This could be your partner, a friend, or a relative, as long as it is someone you can trust. You'll be more able to cope after you've had a break.

3. Don't feel guilty. The fact that she cries every night does not mean you are an inadequate parent. As long as you can eliminate the typical sources of distress, then her tears are probably not related to the way you care for her.

4. Take a long-term view. If your baby cries regularly during her first 15 months, reassure yourself that this is a temporary phase. Crying usually eases off markedly soon after the age of 1 year.

5. Have confidence. Your level of confidence in your parenting skills affects the way you handle your baby; she can sense when you are unsure and tense. So tell yourself that your techniques for soothing her will work. Be positive.

Use your judgment when it comes to deciding whether or not to pick up your crying baby. Be prepared to be flexible; sometimes it may be appropriate to leave her a little longer, whereas at other times what she needs is a reassuring cuddle. It

really is up to you to do what you think is best.

Below: Babies often cry before they go to sleep. As a parent you are best placed to judge whether your baby is in distress or her cries will subside into slumber.

Feeding and Weaning

The decision to either bottle-feed or breast-feed your baby is entirely up to you – choose the method with which you are most comfortable. Whatever method of feeding you select, however, the point will arise when you realize that your baby is still hungry after each feeding and that he needs to eat more than milk alone. And that's when weaning begins, when he progresses from just drinking milk to drinking milk and eating solid food. Although your baby's body is telling him and you that he requires solids, he may find the transition difficult because he is so used to his current method of feeding. Take a planned approach to weaning to help him through this phase.

Early Feeding

Your baby's ability to suck milk from a breast or bottle is instinctive. He is born with two reflexes that make this possible, namely, the sucking reflex (which makes him automatically suck at any object placed in his mouth) and the swallowing reflex (which makes him automatically swallow any fluid in his mouth). Feeding is a completely natural process.

Some parents feed their baby on demand; others do so according to schedule. There are advantages and disadvantages with each method:

Left: Feeding is a natural process.

• **feeding on demand.** The big plus to this technique is that your baby never really has to go hungry – you simply feed him when you think he is ready to eat. You give your baby control over his feeding schedule. The big minus is that you can end up feeding him many times throughout the day and night, without any lengthy break, and one feeding can run into the next. Feeding on demand, however, is widely recommended by health professionals especially when babies are young.

• **feeding on schedule.** On the positive side, feeding him on a fixed schedule enables you to plan your day (and your baby's) more effectively – it gets him used to managing his basic needs. On the negative side, however, the schedule might mean that he is hungry and distressed in between each feeding, and if he isn't satisfied after one feeding he has to wait for the next one.

Left: Once your baby is used to solid food he will enjoy feeding himself. Finger foods are a good starting point.

As with the type of feeding, the feeding strategy itself is your choice. Select the one with which you are most comfortable. Once you have chosen to feed either on schedule or on demand, try to stick with it rather than changing from one to the other and back again. Have confidence in your feeding strategy. Constantly changing from demand to schedule or vice versa can confuse your growing baby.

✦✦✦✦ Top·Tips ✦✦✦✦

1. Relax about feeding. Of course you want your baby to eat enough and of course you are anxious that he should transfer happily from milk alone to solids and milk. But if you are tense during feeding, he'll experience tension, too.

2. Think before you feed. Don't automatically assume that your baby cries between feeding because he is hungry. He could be uncomfortable or bored. Check other possibilities before rushing to organize his next food intake.

3. Make hygiene a priority. Cleanliness is important for both breast- and bottle-feeding. Unfortunately, the combination of your tiredness and the pressure of feeding a hungry baby can quickly result in lapses of hygiene.

4. Persist with weaning. Your baby's initial reaction of distaste to solid food might put you off the whole process. Don't give up so easily. Instead, take a consistent, regular approach when introducing solids into his diet.

5. Encourage your baby. As he takes his first taste of solid foods, let him know that you are delighted with him. Smile at him, talk to him, and give him a big cuddle. This reassures your baby and puts him in a more positive mood.

Weaning

Eventually your baby will reach the stage where he simply can't satisfy his hunger from either breast or formula milk alone. This is because the store of minerals he was born with (for example, iron) begins to run out and he instinctively searches for something more substantial; his body size is also larger and this means he needs more nourishment to keep going.

There's no specific time to wean your baby from milk to solids. If he seems satisfied with milk meals every day then he probably gets all the food intake he requires – certainly he'll not gain any special nutritional benefits from eating solids before the age of 4 months. Let your baby set the pace. If he starts to demand additional feedings or begins to wake more often at night from hunger then he may be ready for solid food. This will probably be between 4 and 6 months.

Do this gradually. To get him used to the new taste, put a tiny amount of solid food on the tip of a clean, plastic baby-sized spoon and put it in his mouth. Remember that your baby is used to tasting only milk and so his face is likely to screw up with displeasure when he first tastes solids. Give him a drink of milk immediately afterward. Later on

Above: By 11 months your baby can enjoy a wide range of foods, and drink from a trainer cup.

during the same feeding, let him taste the solid again, then give him some more milk. In this way, his familiarity with the taste of solid food slowly builds up, as does the amount of solids that he takes with his milk during each feeding.

Right: At 5 months your baby will still need her food puréed, but between 6 and 9 months you can introduce foods with lumpier textures.

Sleeping Patterns

Your baby needs sleep to stay bright, but you'll find that she doesn't always sleep precisely when you want her to. In the first few weeks her sleep pattern is irregular, though by the age of 6 to 8 weeks her naps are more predictable and she starts to sleep for longer periods through the night. Some babies resist sleep at all costs, even when they are tired, whereas others settle down to sleep without any complaint whatsoever. Evidence from psychological surveys confirms that the majority of parents are troubled at some stage because their baby likes to stay awake at night.

Facts About Sleep

Here are some facts about sleeping patterns during your baby's first 15 months:

• your firstborn child is more likely than your other children to have sleep difficulties.

• a baby weaned on to solid foods later than normal is more likely to be a poor sleeper (but early weaning can cause health problems).

• gender difference has no effect on sleeping patterns; boys and girls develop a stable sleeping routine at the same rate.

• it is not until around the age of 3 or 4 months that your baby sleeps more during the night than she does during the day.

• during sleep, your baby's pupils decrease, she breathes less air, her heartbeat slows, and she produces urine at a slower rate.

• your baby needs sleep; if she doesn't sleep well she eventually becomes irritable and moody, and will lose interest in both feeding and playing.

During the early months, your baby probably sleeps in total for about 19

Above: A newborn baby's sleep pattern is unpredictable and will often remain so for the first three or four months.

hours every day, although she sleeps very lightly and at times you may not even notice that she is no longer awake. On average, she will fall asleep up to eight times per day.

Once she is a year old, however, your baby sleeps for only around 13 hours every day. Your own sleep pattern as an adult is quite different from your baby's, so be prepared for early parenthood to be tiring! But don't worry – her sleeping habits will begin to match yours as her first year progresses.

When She Won't Sleep

Your baby's sleep habits are extremely variable during the first four or five weeks, and you may find she sleeps and wakes according to her own timetable, no matter how hard you try to influence her. If you are sure that she is comfortable, well fed, and much loved, then accept her sleeping pattern for what it is because it isn't linked to your management of her.

Right: At night try to resettle your baby without turning on the light or getting her up. Keep the environment as calm and unstimulating as possible to reinforce that nighttime is for sleeping.

Yet there are lots of techniques you can try to help your baby sleep. Every baby is different and what works with your best friend's baby might not work with yours. Some babies nod off when rocked gently or in response to soft background noise, others when wrapped snugly in a blanket or stroked gently. Be prepared to use different techniques when trying to soothe your baby to sleep. You'll eventually find a method that suits her – though that same method might not work with her next week.

If your baby aged 3 months or older wakes up during the night, be sure she is not in pain and doesn't need a

change of diaper, and then try to encourage her to go back to sleep. Don't be tempted to make a big fuss over her, because this is effectively a reward for waking up and she is likely to do the same the next night.

Below: If all else fails, most babies will drop off to sleep in the car.

❖❖❖❖ Top ∙ Tips ❖❖❖❖

1. Check the bedroom for comfort. A pleasantly warm room, that is neither too hot nor stuffy, with subdued lighting creates an atmosphere for sleep. Reduce loud background noise if at all possible.

2. Stick to a routine. Your baby responds best to routine. A regular time for a morning or afternoon nap, and her nighttime sleep, helps her achieve a stable sleeping pattern.

3. Bathe her before bedtime. She'll be soothed and relaxed by a warm bath, a fresh diaper, and a clean change of clothes. Once this routine is complete, place her in her crib and read her a story, using a gentle and relaxed voice tone.

4. Time her naps. It is not always possible to keep your baby awake when she decides to take a nap. Yet she may want to stay awake during the evening and night if she had a long nap just before her last feeding of the day.

5. Don't panic. A baby who lies awake during the night seeking parental attention can exhaust and worry you. But if you let anxiety take you over, this will have a negative effect on your baby, making her even less able to fall asleep.

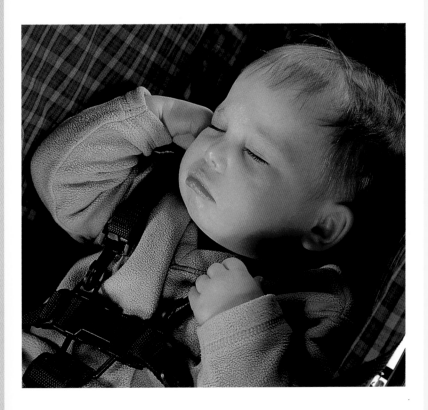

Discipline

The chances are that your baby is wonderful, but there will still be moments when you have to lay down rules for him to follow: for instance, when he grabs the glasses from your face then twists them in his little hands, or when he screams with rage because you won't give him that extra treat. Discipline is not simply about punishment – on the contrary, if punishment forms part of your discipline, it should have a very minor role. Instead, discipline encourages your infant to take control of his own behavior and to think of others. From this perspective, it can only be good for him.

Above: It may sometimes help to calm an upset child if you pick her up and reinforce your point quietly and firmly.

Understanding

Your baby's understanding of discipline develops gradually during the first 15 months. Certainly, there is absolutely no point in accusing a young baby of being naughty, because until the age of 6 months at the earliest he can't possibly understand rules. Likewise, it makes little sense to warn your 3-month-old baby to stop crying or he will be in serious trouble. True, there are some people who tell you that you have to set rules eventually and that

it is better to start the process when your baby is young than to leave it until later when it might be too late. But that's a rather harsh approach. In general, your baby can't begin to grasp the meaning of rules until he has a better grasp of the world around him.

The situation changes, however, during the middle of the first year. Between the ages of 6 and 12 months, he begins to understand when you say the word "no" to him – you can tell this by his negative reaction. The instant he glares at you and deliberately tries to do something that you have told him not to, is the time to take discipline seriously. From that moment onward, the process of establishing rules with him begins.

Right: Uncooperative behavior can often stem from tiredness or frustration rather than deliberate disobedience.

Remember, however, that discipline with your growing baby is not about coercion. In fact, the source of the word "discipline" lies in the Latin word meaning "learning" – in other words, your baby

should learn through discipline. He should not be afraid of it. Try to create a caring atmosphere at home that encourages him to learn rules, rather than a system that tries to force him into good behavior.

Styles of Discipline

You'll make your own decision about the type of discipline you want with your child. A lot will depend on your attitudes, on your childhood memories of the way your own parents established discipline with you, and on the relationship that you and your baby have together. Expect your baby to challenge you occasionally, despite his charming personality. That's a normal part of the learning process. Remind yourself if necessary that he is just the same as every other child, and that you are just as effective as every other parent.

The most common styles of parental discipline are

• **authoritarian.** This type of parent is extremely inflexible: they set rules that have to be followed on every single occasion, without exception. Their baby must conform at all times, and breaches of rules are always punished.

• **democratic.** This type of parent has rules, too, but the rules are fair, they are in the baby's best interests, and they often involve basic safety. Breaches of rules are usually dealt with firmly, but using explanations rather than punishments.

• **permissive.** This type of parent takes a hands-off approach to discipline, based on the assumption that their baby will

Above: Long-term success is more likely to be achieved with a consistent democratic approach to discipline.

learn rules through experience as he grows. There is no punishment because there are no set rules.

Most parents have a mixture of styles with one type dominating. Research suggests that babies and young children don't thrive best in extremes, so authoritarian and permissive styles are rarely the most effective. In providing discipline for your baby, you aim for him to reach the stage of self-discipline in which he doesn't need you to tell him how to behave.

Below: There are times when you need to be very firm to get your message across.

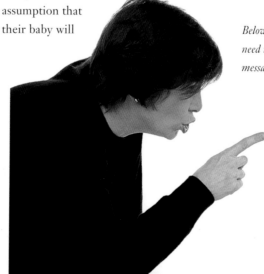

❖❖❖❖ Top·Tips ❖❖❖❖

1. Keep calm. Try to stay calm when your baby or toddler breaks the rules. If you lose your temper with him, he'll just become upset, too, and won't learn anything in that state. Deal with him firmly, but without getting angry.

2. Explain rules to him. You know that, for instance, your 9-month-old baby can't fully understand an explanation about the importance of a particular rule, but say it to him anyway. At some point he will start to grasp its meaning.

3. Avoid physical punishment. Smacking doesn't work as a deterrent and has only a short-term effect. In the long term smacking your toddler makes him frightened of you and may actually make him more defiant and determined.

4. Use positive reinforcement. One of the best ways to encourage your baby or toddler to follow rules is to praise him, cuddle him, and generally show approval when he does behave well. That's better than punishment.

5. Be firm but flexible. For every rule there is an exception. Although you should usually stand your ground, there are also times when you can let your toddler misbehave without reprimand, perhaps because he is just overexcited.

Confidence

The foundations of your child's self-confidence are laid during the first year. She may only be a young baby, but she already has a sense of self, a sense of what she can and cannot do. Her confidence is affected by the achievements she makes: for instance, when at the age of 3 months she manages to reach out and grasp a toy that attracts her attention, or at the age of 1 year when she takes her first step. The way others react toward her affect her confidence – your love, praise, and interest all boost your baby's belief in herself.

Components of Confidence

Self-confidence has a significant effect on your baby's development because it influences her motivation, her drive to achieve, and her relationships with others. There are three aspects of your baby's confidence to consider:

• **self-belief.** This is the extent to which she believes that she has the ability to master the challenges that face her. A baby who has little self-belief won't even try to play with a new toy because she thinks that it will be too difficult for her; as a result she would rather lie passively in her familiar crib than run the risk of failure.

• **self-value.** This is the extent to which your baby values herself, and can be seen during the

Left: Your encouragement and support will help your child gain the confidence to take her first steps.

Right: A reassuring hug can make all the difference at times when your child is upset.

first year. Watch your baby trying to achieve something; when she does, she will probably turn to you and give you a huge grin. In contrast, a baby with a low level of self-value is unimpressed with her own achievements.

• **self-reflection.** This is the extent to which your baby receives positive

feedback from other people around her. When you tell your baby how much you love her and give her a big cuddle because, say, she managed to sit up on her own, this gives her a positive self-reflection, making her feel good about herself.

A baby with low self-confidence has less enjoyment in life, prefers to take a more passive role, and may have difficulty giving love and receiving it from others. Challenge and adventure threaten her rather than excite her, making her reluctant to discover and learn.

A Head Start

Findings from psychological research suggest that the typical baby under the age of 15 months has a very strong belief in her own abilities. That's why she is willing to explore and venture into new areas – she believes there is no challenge that is beyond her. It's almost as though your young baby has an innate positive sense of self-belief; she's already programmed for stimulation.

This positive self-belief extends to most areas of her life. For instance, she'll try to reach for a new toy that attracts her attention, she'll try to move her body across the floor when she wants to get to the other side of the room, and she'll try to communicate with you even though she has barely started babbling. In other words, she's born ready and raring to go!

Yet her belief in herself is easily dented by experience. The sudden realization that, for example, she can't move the rattle in a way that creates a noise can dampen her interest in the toy. The same thing can happen when your baby tries to crawl across the floor, discovers that she hasn't moved very far, and then howls in frustration. If failure of this sort occurs often enough, your baby's self-confidence dips and she'll give up trying.

So watch her closely when she plays. Give her the freedom to play on her own so that she experiences the success of achievement, but be ready to step in if you see frustration and disappointment building up. If your baby does lose her temper or let frustration get the better of her, cuddle her, cheer her up, and direct her toward another toy or activity that you know she has already mastered. She can always return to the original activity later on when she is in a more positive frame of mind.

Right: At 15 months this little boy's whole manner radiates self-confidence and independence.

❖❖❖ Top ❖ Tips ❖❖❖

1. Have plenty of loving physical contact. A warm, loving hug is a fundamental way of telling your baby that you love her and think she is marvelous. Contact of this sort with you boosts her self-belief.

2. Reassure her. If she explodes with frustration because, for instance, she can't switch on the music box, try to calm her. Reassure her that she'll soon learn how to do it, and then let her see you turn the switch for her.

3. Break challenges into small stages. Your baby wants to do everything, even when the task is clearly beyond her. Help her complete the activity in stages. It's easier to crawl a few inches, for example, than to reach the other side of the room.

4. Tell your baby what you feel about her. Although she can't understand the literal meaning of your words, she can read your nonverbal communication, such as your positive facial expression and happy voice tone.

5. Avoid obvious pitfalls. There is no point in deliberately letting your baby learn through failure. If you can see she is heading for a disappointment, steer her away from that activity before she fully embarks on it.

Special Needs

Estimates suggest that up to one baby in five has special needs – in other words, his development does not follow the typical pattern. For instance, his speech might not develop at the same rate as other children his age, he may still not have taken his first step long after his peers are steady on their feet, or he might not understand how a particular toy works even though it has been designed for use by his age group. A baby with special needs has exactly the same psychological needs as any baby, but his needs are different when it comes to stimulation.

Identification

Some difficulties with development, such as Down's syndrome or spina bifida, are usually detected at birth, whereas others may not be spotted until later, perhaps because the baby doesn't start to talk at the time he is expected to or because his understanding seems less advanced than would typically be expected of a child his age. If you have any doubts at all about your baby's development, speak to your pediatrician. The chances are that you have no need to be worried, but you'll feel reassured by an opinion from someone else.

The developmental checklists given later in this chapter (see pages 38–47) offer a guide to typical progress made during the first 15 months. Do remember, however, that if your baby does not pass the stages

at the suggested times, it does not mean he has special needs. The chances are that he'll be ready to progress to the next skill very soon. Give your baby time to develop his potential.

Each parent reacts in his/her own way on realizing his/her baby has special needs. Research shows that once the initial impact of the news has passed, most parents cope well. Some blame themselves even though they are clearly not at fault. It's helpful to share the feelings you experience with a friend or partner who can lend you a sympathetic, understanding ear.

The Importance of Play

Your baby with special needs still learns through play – it's as important to him as to any other child. However, he may need extra help to get the most out of the stimulation you provide for him. Monitor his play patterns and his reactions to toys and other activities.

Right: Whether your baby has special needs or not, your input has a vital part to play in helping her reach her full potential.

Left: Toys such as stacking rings may be complicated for your baby but with encouragement and involvement from you, he will progress.

1. Emphasize similarities, not differences. Keep thinking about all the similarities between your baby and other babies, instead of focusing on the differences. Your baby is very special and he thrives best when you have an upbeat attitude.

2. Have sensible discipline. Parents of a baby with special needs are less likely to establish discipline with him than with their other children. Yet he needs to have rules laid down and limits set on his behavior, in exactly the same way as the others.

3. Gather information. The more you know about the difficulty with your baby's development, the better. Read about it, talk to the professionals involved with your baby, and listen to the experiences of other parents, too.

4. Value his achievements. Compared with other babies who seem to be progressing at a rapid rate, your baby's achievements may appear relatively minor. But to him they are huge, and he benefits from your enthusiasm at each bit of progress.

5. Be patient and persist. You might feel frustrated and disappointed about your baby's slow progress, but persist with your stimulation activities despite this lack of feedback. Your patience will be rewarded.

Take a positive outlook. For every difficulty and hurdle your baby comes across when playing, there is a practical solution. For instance, if he

• **lacks the normal level of curiosity that you would expect in a young baby,** then make more of an effort to stimulate his interest by showing him a wider array of toys and by playing with him for longer periods of time.

• **has limited concentration and loses interest very quickly,** then play with him for shorter periods but have more of them during the day. His concentration is sharper when he uses it in shorter bursts.

• **has weak hand control and can't hold toys properly in his fingers,** then gently ease his fingers open, place the toy in the palm of his hand, and gently wrap his fingers around it. This procedure will give him the feeling of opening and closing his hands.

• **is still unable to sit up independently because his back strength has not progressed,** then either prop him on the floor by surrounding him with cushions, or place him in a supported chair so that he can sit upright.

• **has slower physical development that is restricting his ability to move to the other side of the room,** then identify the objects that attract his attention and bring them over to him. This will overcome the learning limitation placed on him by his physical ability.

It's a case of getting to know your baby's individual strengths and weaknesses and developing play and discovery strategies that are appropriate for him. Although his progress may be slower than you might expect, he will steadily advance and improve his abilities during these first 15 months. He needs lots of stimulation.

Below: You will be able to stimulate your baby's interest more easily by using a wide range of toys in your play.

Development
First Week Skills

Movement
- Sucks in reflex when a soft object is placed in his mouth.
- Automatically swallows milk on his tongue.
- If startled he will arch his back and throw his arms and legs in the air (Moro reflex).
- Moves legs in a reflex stepping action if his feet are lowered onto a flat surface.
- When his cheek is stroked he turns his head to find the nipple ("rooting" reflex).
- He cannot hold his head without support or raise it from the mattress.
- While sleeping he often lies with arms and legs in the fetal position.

Hand–Eye Coordination
- Grasps items placed in his hand in a reflex reaction but is unable to hold onto them.
- Focuses on an object that is roughly 8–10 inches from his face.
- Often holds his hand in a fist.
- Blinks in reflex when an object approaches his face quickly.

First Month Skills

Movement
- She can raise her head a couple of inches when lying facedown.
- Moves her head from side to side but mostly lies with her right cheek on the mattress.
- Kicks her arms and legs in the air.
- Screws up her face when she experiences a bitter taste.
- Tries to turn onto her side when lying on her back.
- When startled will still arch her back and fling out her arms and legs in the Moro reflex action.

Hand–Eye Coordination
- Stares at objects about 8–10 inches from her face.
- She will follow objects that are moved a few inches from side to side.
- Moves her hands without much control but can connect her fist with her mouth.
- She may pull her blanket toward her.
- The grasp reflex is still strong when something is placed in her palm.

Language
- Uses a wider range of cries, and parents can begin to distinguish the difference between cries of hunger, boredom,

Second Month Skills

Movement
- Limited control over arms and legs.
- Holds a small object for a few moments.
- Holds his head off the mattress for a couple of seconds.
- Neck control increases and is beginning to support the weight of his head when he is carried.
- Early reflexes (Moro, grasp reflex) are fading.

Hand–Eye Coordination
- Hand control begins; his hands are mostly open with fingers becoming more flexible.
- Peers with interest at his fingers.
- The grasp reflex fades.
- He will close his fingers around a small object placed in his palm and move the object toward his face.
- Tries but cannot reach accurately for a small toy.

Language
- Makes a cooing, repetitive vowel sound when relaxed.
- Uses a couple of identifiable but meaningless sounds.
- Becomes quiet when he is lifted up.
- Moves his eyes to look for the source of a noise.
- Watches the gestures and body language of those talking to him.

Third Month Skills

Movement
- Improved head control means she can hold her head off the mattress for longer whether lying on tummy or back.
- Enjoys being held upright, and head and neck movements become more varied.
- Leg movements become quite vigorous when kicking.
- Better at moving her body around her crib.

Hand–Eye Coordination
- Watches an object as it moves around the room.
- Stretches out her hand toward an object close to her.
- Grabs a toy firmly when it is placed in her hand.
- Thrusts her hands toward source of food.
- Will stare at pictures in books and try to touch them.
- Peers at objects and tries to put them in her mouth to explore their properties.

Language
- More attentive to distinctive sounds she hears.
- Listening skills have improved and she goes quiet when she hears a small noise.
- Enjoys hearing you sing to her.
- Gurgles and coos in response to sounds;

From Birth to 3 Months

Language
- Tries to look at you when you speak to him.
- Reacts to sounds such as a sudden noise.
- Recognizes his parent's voice and can distinguish high and low pitches.
- Makes eye contact if held close to your face.

Learning
- Is able to focus his attention on you.
- Can distinguish the faces of his parents from those of strangers.
- Recognizes his parents' scent within days.
- Is sensitive to touch and is calmed by being held.
- Has varying periods of alertness but sleeps 80 percent of the day in about eight naps.

Social and Emotional
- Enjoys your company and responds positively to your voice.
- Stares at your face when it is within 8–10 inches of his.
- Cries when he is unhappy or uncomfortable.
- Moves his arms and legs around in excitement.

tiredness, discomfort.
- Conveys mood through agitated arm and leg movements, and facial expressions such as mouth twitching or staring.
- She makes sounds when she is happy.
- Responds positively to soothing words.

Learning
- Loves to look at anything in her surroundings.

- Will stare for longer at blue and green objects than red ones.
- Is fascinated by objects placed near her.
- She will remember an object that reappears within a few seconds of moving.
- Begins to recognize your voice as distinct from others.
- She is alert for about one in every ten hours.

Social and Emotional
- Enjoys a cuddle and being smiled at.
- Responds positively when you talk and sing to her.
- Makes eye contact.
- Is able to relax at bathtime, kicking and splashing in the water.
- Cries from hunger, thirst, discomfort.
- May mimic if you stick your tongue out at her.

- Is encouraged to repeat sounds when people smile and talk back to him.

Learning
- Can control vision more accurately and peers at an object moved in a pattern in front of him.
- Likes listening to music and is comforted by background sounds such as the washing machine or car engine.

- Becomes excited in anticipation, for example when he sees the bath.
- Begins to coordinate his senses by looking toward sounds.
- Clearly distinguishes between people, voices, tastes.

Social and Emotional
- He has shown you his first smile and is likely to smile if you beam at him.

- Enjoys attention from you and others.
- Stays awake for longer if people interact with him.
- May begin to sleep through the night.
- Begins to amuse himself when left alone by looking around, tracking and batting at objects.
- Feeding becomes a social experience: he looks at you while you feed and talk to him.

will gurgle to herself for several minutes.
- Makes at least two distinct sounds such as "oooh" and "aaah."

Learning
- Sees a link between her hand movement and the toy's reaction; for example a toy might rattle when she moves it.
- Improved memory allows her to anticipate events such as feeding, and reappearance

of a person playing peek-a-boo.
- Recognizes familiar music.
- Will imitate actions such as opening and closing mouth, sticking out her tongue.
- Fascinated by her hands, which she fans in front of her face.
- Begins to differentiate family members by sight and the sound of their voice.
- Can tell the difference between a woman's face and a man's face.

Social and Emotional
- More responsive to any adult who shows interest in her.
- Thrives on attention, even tries to attract attention when a parent is near her.
- Has a broad range of facial expressions to express her moods.
- Smiles a lot more readily, and her crying decreases.

Development
Fourth Month Skills

Movement
- Sits in an upright position with support.
- Turns from left side to right, and vice versa, without help.
- May start to roll over from front to back and vice versa.
- Pulls himself around the crib.
- Head doesn't flop around when you hold him.
- Can turn and move his head in all directions.
- Grasping is deliberate and no longer a reflex.

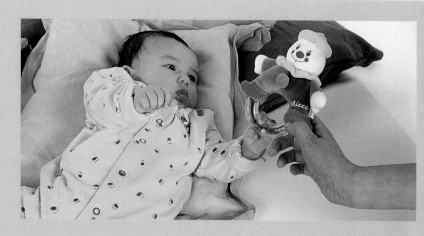

Fifth Month Skills

Movement
- Pushes feet firmly against surfaces such as the bottom of the crib.
- Moves around the floor by rolling and turning her body.
- Can keep her legs in the air and kick them about freely.
- Holds her head confidently when she is supported in an upright position.

Hand–Eye Coordination
- Watches you as you move around the room.
- Starts to look for an object that has slipped from her grasp.
- Lifts her hand toward a nearby object and reaches for it more accurately than before.
- Can hold a small toy in her hand.
- Has a firm grip and doesn't like to let go.

Sixth Month Skills

Movement
- Sits up on his own without requiring any support.
- Pushes his head, chest, and shoulders off the floor when facedown.
- Shows first signs of crawling by drawing one knee to his tummy.
- Makes energetic body movements to propel himself on the floor.
- Becoming more adept at rolling from front to back and back to front.
- Twists and turns in all directions.

Hand–Eye Coordination
- Uses both hands in synchrony and can pass objects from one hand to the other.
- Keeps watching a toy that falls from his grip.
- Plays with toys more purposefully instead of just mouthing them.
- Enjoys dropping a toy and picking it up again repeatedly.
- Tries to feed himself by putting food to his mouth with his fingers.
- Grabs hold of the bottle or spoon while having his meal.

Language
- Synchronizes his speech with yours as though in conversation.
- Produces more different vowel and consonant sounds such as f, v, ka, da, ma.
- Laughs when happy and now screams when angry.
- Makes gurgling noises when playing contentedly.
- Begins to react to the mood of music that he hears.

From 4 to 6 Months

Hand–Eye Coordination
• Reaches out when you place him in the bath and slaps his hand in the water.
• Tries to grab objects near him.
• Stares at the place from which an object has dropped.
• Waves small toys held in his hand.
• His eyesight has improved and he can focus on near and distant objects as well as an adult can.

Language
• Gives a definite laugh when something entertains or amuses him.
• Makes vocalizations to attract your attention.
• Listens keenly to distinct noises.
• Shows pleasure through excited movement and delighted facial expressions.

Learning
• Recalls how to play with a familiar toy in a particular way.
• Peers at his own reflection in a mirror.

• Looks curiously at objects.
• May take two or three naps in the day, and can be alert for up to an hour at a time.

Social and Emotional
• Uses facial expressions to keep your attention.
• Chuckles spontaneously when he feels happy.
• Enjoys familiar situations such as feeding, bathing, dressing.
• Laughs loudly when he is tickled.
• Relaxes when you sing gently to him.

Language
• Makes an increased range of sounds with consonants such as d, m, b.
• Uses three or four babbling sounds at random, combining vowels and consonants; for example, "nanana."
• Vocalizes when you talk to her and may babble to you during gaps in your speaking.
• May imitate your facial expressions and observes your reaction to her.
• Tries to imitate sounds she hears.
• Listens intently and can hear almost as well as an adult.

Learning
• Likes to explore whenever she has the opportunity.
• Focuses well but prefers to look at objects within 3 feet of her.
• Is curious enough to handle any object near to her.
• Detects a sound source accurately by turning toward it.
• Drops one object when another attracts her interest.
• Weaning begins with the introduction of solid foods.

Social and Emotional
• May form an attachment to a cuddly toy or other comforter and likes to have this object close to her when going to sleep.
• Can play on her own for short periods.
• Shows interest in new surroundings.
• Complains when you try to remove a toy from her hand.
• Can be shy in the company of strangers.
• Smiles and vocalizes to attract attention.

Learning
• Recognizes himself in a photograph or mirror.
• Switches his stare from one object to another as though comparing them.
• Holds a toy in each hand without dropping them.
• Actively reaches out for toys that attract his curiosity.
• May start to understand the meaning of "no."
• Can differentiate between men and women by their voice tones.

Social and Emotional
• May become anxious in strange company and begin to cry.
• Chuckles in anticipation when you come toward him.
• Playfully holds onto a toy when you try to remove it.
• Coos or stops crying in response to familiar music.
• Turns when he hears his own name.
• Becomes anxious in some situations, for example when he has maneuvered himself into an awkward position.

Development

Seventh Month Skills

Movement
- Rolls competently from back to front and vice versa.
- More consistently draws one knee toward her tummy in a crawling movement.
- May be able to move along the floor with her tummy raised.
- Takes her own weight when supported under her arms.
- Often brings feet to her mouth to suck on her toes.

Hand–Eye Coordination
- Explores toys in new and interesting ways, by rattling, shaking, and banging them.
- Pulls at different parts of a toy.
- Has a good firm grasp and is less likely to drop a held object.
- Is more accurate when using her fingers to feed herself.
- Begins to use finger and thumb in a pincer movement.
- Uses her hands to explore her own and other faces.

Eighth Month Skills

Movement
- Has improved leg and foot strength so tries more adventurous balancing.
- Takes his own weight, gripping a chair for support.
- Able to crawl forward and backward.
- Pulls himself to standing, although he finds it hard work.

Hand–Eye Coordination
- Uses finger and thumb together in a pincer grip.
- Opens and closes hands voluntarily.

Ninth Month Skills

Movement
- Can turn around while crawling.
- Moves her entire body comfortably around the room.
- Makes a stepping response when held under the arms.
- Shows interest in climbing up stairs.

Hand–Eye Coordination
- Uses a firm pincer movement to feed herself finger food such as peas and raisins.
- Hand movements are more coordinated: she may be able to build a two-brick tower.
- Brings her hands together deliberately.

From 7 to 9 Months

Language
• More responsive when you talk to her and will respond to comments such as "Look at that."
• Likes to hear songs and to babble along with them.
• Seems to understand your different voice tones, such as happy, serious, surprised.
• Has a clear understanding of a firm "no."
• Enjoys blowing "raspberries."

Learning
• Remembers faces of familiar adults she does not see very frequently, such as a baby-sitter.
• Continues to look for an object that goes out of her vision.
• Knows how to move toys to make them noisy.
• Understands that she can make objects move.

Social and Emotional
• Lets you know when she's miserable or happy.
• Gets annoyed if you stop her from doing something.
• Is very aware of verbal praise and enthusiasm.
• Skilled at attracting attention when she's bored.
• Enjoys the familiarity of routines such as bathtime and bedtime.

• Likes to drop objects when sitting in his high chair.
• Tries to pull at a string attached to a toy.

Language
• Tries to imitate the sounds you make.
• Repeats the same sound over and over, such as syllables of words you use.
• Opens and closes his mouth when he watches you eat, imitating your jaw action.
• Shouts to attract your attention.

Learning
• Looks for a concealed object.
• Facial expression shows he recognizes a toy not seen for a couple of weeks.
• Plays with two or more toys together.
• Curious about new items.
• Discovers new properties in familiar toys: the ball he chews will roll away if pushed.
• Makes an effort to reach objects some distance away.
• Begins to mimic actions such as waving.
• Is alert for longer and may manage with only one nap during the day.

Social and Emotional
• Initiates social contact with other adults.
• Clings to you in crowded places.
• May be shy and reluctant to be picked up by strangers.
• Fascinated by mirror images and family photographs.
• Enjoys being in presence of other babies but does not play cooperatively with them.
• May answer simple questions by facial expression, body movements, and sounds.

• Scans her surroundings and attends to small details.
• She may be able to point to an object she wants.

Language
• Uses two-syllable babbles consistently, such as "dada," "mama."
• Says her first word, though it may be unclear.
• Listens when you speak to her and can understand simple instructions such as "Come here."
• Will interrupt play to find the source of a particular sound such as a ringing bell.
• May be able to imitate animal sounds you make to her.

Learning
• Loves to feel the texture of objects.
• Arranges small toys into different patterns and shapes.
• Bangs two small toys together to make sounds.
• Waves her hands in response to someone waving at her.
• Enjoys familiar games and rhymes and laughs at appropriate times.

• Makes connections between actions; for example, if she pulls the rug the toy on it will come closer.

Social and Emotional
• Is curious about other babies her own age and may stare or poke at another child.
• Covers her toys if another child approaches.
• Gets upset when she sees that you or other children are upset.
• Looks up at you as she plays on the floor.
• Reacts to an audience and will repeat an action that is applauded.

Development
Tenth Month Skills

Movement
- Likes looking at the world from an upright position.
- Good at crawling and able to propel himself along the floor.
- Climbs up the first step and slides down from it.
- Stands on his own two feet, gripping something for support.

Hand–Eye Coordination
- Likes playing with toys that move across the floor.
- Likes to explore boxes, cupboards, and drawers.
- Grips two small blocks in one hand.
- Hand preference may begin to show.
- Enjoys rhymes involving hand coordination such as "Pat-a-Cake."

Language
- Combines different syllables in one utterance, for example "ah-leh," "muh-gah."
- Stops what he is doing and listens when you say his name.
- Says one or two words consistently, not always clearly.
- Chatters in the rhythm of speech but without meaning.
- Moves his body along to the rhythm of music.

Eleventh Month Skills

Movement
- Moves swiftly around the room, supporting herself with the furniture.
- Slowly and gently lowers herself to the ground, landing with only a small bump.
- May bottom-shuffle around the room.
- May lean toward an object on the floor while standing against support.

Hand–Eye Coordination
- Is fascinated by containers and shakes them in the air.
- Tries to pull lids off boxes to find whatever is inside them.
- Shows good coordination of thumb and index finger.
- Turns pages of a book as you sit with her.
- Enjoys putting one thing into another.
- May be able to build a small tower of stacking cups or blocks.

Language
- Listens to you very carefully when you talk to her.
- Follows simple instructions, for instance to give things to you and take them back.
- Occasionally utters single words but much of her language appears meaningless.
- Enjoys playing with musical toys and experimenting with her own sounds to accompany these.
- Will point to an object in a picture book when you say its name.

Twelfth Month Skills

Movement
- Shows the early signs of independent walking.
- More confident climbing up the stairs.
- Has better body control when lowering himself from standing.
- Crawls effectively on his hands and knees.
- May walk if you hold his hands or when he is pushing a wheeled toy.

Hand–Eye Coordination
- May use a spoon for stirring rather than banging.
- Spends time building with small wooden blocks.
- Enjoys water games and can pour from containers held in either left or right hand.
- Can slot simple shapes correctly into a shape-sorter.
- May be able to make a mark on paper with a crayon.
- Hand preference is more obvious.

From 10 to 12 Months

Learning

- Tries to imitate your actions.
- Is interested in things that go together, such as cup and saucer and parts of puzzles.
- Listens to and follows basic instructions such as "Give me the cup."
- Likes trying to push shapes into a shape-sorter.
- Spends up to a fifth of his waking time staring and observing.

Social and Emotional

- Gives cuddles as well as receiving them.
- Loves interactive games, like peek-a-boo.
- Is happy to spend time amusing himself.
- May be anxious when visiting unfamiliar places.
- Snuggles up to you when you read him a story.
- Has no understanding of the effect of his actions on other children.

Learning

- With better concentration she can focus on an activity for at least a minute.
- Can place a small block in a plastic cup.
- Imitates more of your actions as you move around the house.
- Tries something, then reflects on her actions for a few moments.
- May attempt the next action in a familiar routine that you have begun.

Social and Emotional

- Is frustrated when her wishes are blocked and loses her temper quite easily.
- Swings from positive to negative moods very quickly.
- Stares at other children but does not interact with them.
- Likes to do things that gain your approval.
- Feels very secure with you but anxious with unfamiliar people.

Language

- Has said his first word: "Dada" is commonly first, or "bye-bye."
- May be able to use three or four words to name familiar objects, for example "dog."
- Follows basic instructions consistently.
- Has good hearing but loses interest in repetitive sounds.
- Knows the names of other members of the family.

Learning

- Understands basic directions involving one familiar action, for example "Wave bye-bye."
- Copies you when you bang two wooden blocks together.
- Is curious about objects that rattle when shaken.
- Makes a good effort to put the pieces of an inset board in place.
- May hesitate when given a new puzzle but will then apply existing knowledge.
- Needs less sleep and may be awake for about 11 hours every day.

Social and Emotional

- Plays any games that involve social interaction between you and him.
- Is very affectionate toward you and others in his family.
- May show temper when he doesn't want to cooperate.
- Has a preference for playing with a child of his own gender when in mixed groups.
- Will play next to another baby his age, but will play actively with an older child.
- Has tremendous belief in his own abilities and is increasingly frustrated when he finds he can't achieve his goals.

Development

Thirteenth Month Skills

Movement
• Spends a lot of time trying to climb up stairs but finds coming down is harder.
• Steadier on her feet, though still topples easily.
• Might rely on a chair or wheeled toy for support when walking.
• Is determined to walk on her own, despite frequent falls.

Hand–Eye Coordination
• Uses her hand to indicate to you that she wants a particular object.

Fourteenth Month Skills

Movement
• Totters about the house, tripping over objects on the floor.
• Is able to stop and change direction when walking.
• Insists on walking unaided when outside with you.
• Climbs stairs on all fours or by shifting his bottom one step at a time.
• May still crawl occasionally although he can walk.

Hand–Eye Coordination
• Knows how to use crayons appropriately instead of mouthing them.
• Can build a tower of two or three bricks.
• Is more adept at fitting difficult pieces into a shape-sorter.
• Puts his hands and arms up when you bring his pullover toward him.
• May be able to throw a medium-sized, lightweight ball.

Fifteenth Month Skills

Movement
• Moves confidently through the house.
• Has better balance as she walks, keeping her arms closer to her sides.
• Can stop when walking and bend to pick up an object from the floor.
• Attempts to stand still and kick a ball if encouraged to do so – but she will probably miss or fall backward, though she still enjoys trying.
• Masters the challenge of climbing in and out of her high chair.
• May be able to kneel on a chair while at a table.

From 13 to 15 Months

- Enjoys making marks on paper with crayons and pencils.
- Hits pegs into a Peg-Board with a hammer.
- Plays with a toy telephone, putting the receiver on and off it.

Language
- Recognizes her own name but probably cannot say it.
- Says five or six words in the appropriate context.
- Shouts out at you when she doesn't

like what you are doing.
- Makes tuneful sounds when hearing familiar music.

Learning
- Will try to use a spoon to feed herself.
- Has fun pointing to pictures of familiar objects in books.
- Will concentrate for longer periods on puzzle toys.
- Interested in videotapes and television programs.
- Begins to show imagination in play.

Social and Emotional
- Innate desire to become independent begins to show; for example, she tries to help when being dressed.
- Is less inclined to go for an afternoon nap.
- Will give you a big cuddle when she is happy.
- Holds a cup and drinks from it, with some help.
- May pass toys to another child.
- Plays alongside rather than with a child of her age.

Language
- Tries to sing along with you.
- Begins to learn the names of body parts.
- Listens avidly to other children when they talk to each other.
- Enjoys making sounds with musical instruments.
- His babbling has all the rhythm of language.
- Is fascinated by the language use of other children the same age.

Learning
- Can complete a simple but lengthy task with encouragement.
- Can look away from what he is doing, then go back to it.
- Is eager to explore the whole house but is oblivious to danger.
- Has a serious facial expression while you read him a story.
- Is developing the use of imagination in play, for example with pretend tea parties.

Social and Emotional
- Is more socially confident yet is sometimes terrified of strangers.
- Has increased sense of self and awareness that he is an individual with his own likes and dislikes.
- Recognizes that his name is different from other people's.
- May develop a minor fear, for example of animals.
- Loves to be independent.
- May have a temporary phase of attachment to one parent in particular.

Hand–Eye Coordination
- Is able to hold two items in each hand at the same time.
- Has a firm hand grip and rarely drops objects accidentally.
- Likes playing with moving objects, watching them as they roll.
- Enjoys fitting pieces into an inset-board puzzle.

Language
- Can say five or six single words.
- Understands many more words than she can say.

- Has great fun when you recite familiar rhymes and songs to her.
- Can follow a broader range of basic instructions: "Let go of the toy," "Take the cookie."

Learning
- Concentrates well until she completes an activity.
- Enjoys pretend play, either alone or with you.
- Will try to put away her toys if instructed to do so.
- Enjoys sand and water play.

Social and Emotional
- Is very determined to get her own way.
- Has a tantrum when her frustrations become too much.
- Wants to feed herself though can't manage entirely on her own.
- Is eager to explore everything whether it is safe or not.
- Begins to show signs of jealousy when you give attention to others.
- Loves the social nature of a family meal.
- Can begin to learn social skills such as greeting another person by saying "hello."

Movement

The Development of Movement

Your baby's transformation from an infant who has almost no control over his head, hand, leg, and body movements at birth into someone who has probably taken his first step by the fifteenth month is one of the most visible signs of development you will ever see. The enormous progress in physical maturity that occurs during this very short period in your baby's life is visibly striking.

Above: A newborn baby has surprising strength, though her movements are random.

What is even more amazing is that some of the remarkable changes in your baby's control over his movements seem to occur spontaneously, without any prompting, alongside his physical and neurological maturation. Take that all-important first step. No matter what you do to encourage him to walk early, he won't be able to do it until he is in a natural state of physical readiness; walking is one of those movement skills that you can't really hurry along. No matter how much walking practice you give a baby who is, say, 4 months old, he won't be able to coordinate his leg and

Right: Once your baby can support her upper body on her arms she is part of the way toward crawling.

body movements at that age to enable him to walk.

In contrast to the skill of walking, there is evidence that practice in other aspects of movement does have an impact. A child who is allowed lots of opportunities to crawl will probably be better at crawling than a child who is denied this form of activity. The same applies to moving up and down stairs. Perhaps the best strategy to take when it comes to encouraging your infant's movement is to

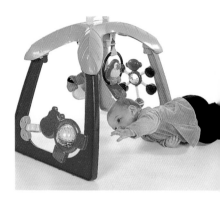

Above: At 6 months your baby may be able to shuffle or roll to reach what he wants.

remember that the pace of his physical and neurological development has a big influence and that this will limit the effect of practice in some areas.

Of course, the blueprint for walking is present almost at birth. If you hold your newborn baby firmly under his arms (while gently supporting his head with your thumbs) and lower the soles of his feet onto a flat surface, he will automatically move

his legs in a reflex stepping action. This looks as though he is walking but he is not. Yet within the next 12 months, this innate, involuntary reaction becomes part of his deliberately controlled movements.

Direction of Control

Every baby is different in terms of rates of movement development, but in general, your baby's ability to gain control over his body movements in the first 15 months follows two distinct directions:

• **from the head down.** He establishes control at the top of his body before lower down. For instance, he will be able to hold his head up independently before his spine is strong enough for him to sit up on his own, and he will sit upright long before he can walk.

• **from the chest out.** Your baby gains control over the middle of his body before his hands and feet. For instance, he can raise his chest off the floor before he can reach out accurately with his hands, and he will be able to pick up something with his fingers before he can kick a ball with his toes.

Scientific research suggests that these two directions in movement development match the sequence of your baby's brain development. In other words, the part of the brain

that is responsible for his head and chest control grows faster than the part of the brain in charge of his arm and leg movements – hence the two-directional pattern in movement progress.

It's also interesting when you consider that movement control develops in a sequence that builds up logically toward the ability to walk. An infant who didn't have, say, control over his head and who couldn't hold it upright would not be able to walk even if his legs were strong enough. In the same way, your baby needs chest and hip control in order to balance while walking or he would topple over. So he's learning to walk long before he stands on his own two feet. In fact, the moment your newborn baby tries to lift his head to see what's going on around him, he has started a developmental sequence that will eventually lead to your buying him his first pair of shoes!

His Own Way

Another amazing aspect of movement in babies is that although the majority of them pass their physical milestones at roughly the same age (for instance, most can sit up on their own by the age of 6 months), there is huge variation in the way that each stage is achieved.

Above: At 15 months this little boy has mastered the complex maneuver of sitting on a chair.

Crawling and walking are good examples of this. Your baby might be one of those who like to crawl with their hands and knees touching the floor, whereas your best friend's infant of the same age might prefer to crawl with his bottom high in the air and his knees raised off the ground. But they are both crawling, in their own distinctive ways. There are even some babies who dislike crawling so much that they show no interest in it, and make a smooth transition from sitting to walking with almost no crawling in between. The same applies with walking. Your baby might have gone from sitting up, to crawling, to standing, to walking. Yet there are other infants who have an intermediate stage of bottom-shuffling in that they sit upright on the floor, gently raising and dropping their bottom as they propel themselves along.

Allow your baby to find his own way of expressing his innate desire to gain control over his body movements. Don't be alarmed if he does not follow the exact same pattern of movement development as others his own age. They usually all get there in the end anyway.

Movement

Age	Skill
1 week	She wants to see the world from different positions but hasn't got sufficient control to raise her head from the mattress or to move onto her side.
1 month	Much to her delight, her head control has developed to the point where she can raise her face when lying in the prone position (facedown).
2 months	She has very limited control over her arms and legs but enough to move them in a very general way when she wants to.
3 months	Her head control is much more mature than before, whether she is lying on her tummy or on her back, giving her a better view of her surroundings.
4 months	Increased back strength allows your baby to start to sit in an upright position, though she can't do this without some form of support.
5 months	Now that her leg and feet muscles are stronger, she is able to push them firmly against any object within their reach.
6 months	At this age most children are able to sit up on their own for the first time without requiring support of any kind.
7 months	In addition to being able to roll from side to side, your growing child may begin to demonstrate the first signs of crawling.

From Birth to 7 Months

What to Do

When you lift up your new baby from her crib, hold the lower part of her body gently but firmly in one hand while gently supporting her head in the other. Raise her with both hands at the same time so that her little head doesn't lag behind her body.

When she is lying facedown in the crib, put your head close to her so that if she raised her head, she would stare right into your face. Then softly say her name and beam at her – she'll lift her head for a couple of seconds to look at you.

Lay your baby on her back in the crib. When she is comfortable, smile at her, and make a noise to indicate that you are excited to see her. In response, she will kick her arms and legs vigorously. This is her way of telling you she is having great fun.

Lay a comfortable blanket on the floor and gently place your baby on it, faceup. Once she is relaxed in that position, hold her hands in yours as though you are about to pull her up. She will start to raise her head firmly in anticipation of being lifted by you.

Seat her on a steady nonslip surface, with her legs straight out in front of her, spread in a V-shape. If you give her back support, she will be able to sit in that position. If she turns too quickly, though, her head may wobble about.

When she is lying in her crib with her feet raised in the air, put the palms of your hands against her soles and hold that position. She will probably push her feet so hard against your hands that her body slides away from you toward the opposite end of the crib.

Sit on the floor with your infant and position her beside you until she is in a stable seated position. Prop cushions around her, because she may topple over. She will hold her head firmly and can turn around confidently if something attracts her attention.

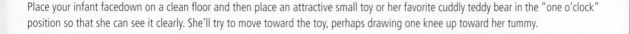

Place your infant facedown on a clean floor and then place an attractive small toy or her favorite cuddly teddy bear in the "one o'clock" position so that she can see it clearly. She'll try to move toward the toy, perhaps drawing one knee up toward her tummy.

Movement

Age	Skill
8 months	Her improved leg and foot strength gives her the confidence to try more adventurous balancing movements.
9 months	Her crawling movements are more coordinated, and she begins to be able to move her entire body.
10 months	Some children this age show determination to view their surroundings from the upright position.
11 months	The world is her oyster now that she can propel herself along the floor without depending on your help.
1 year	For many children – though certainly not all – the early signs of independent walking start to show through.
13 months	Flights of stairs have fascinated her for months, but her increased physical maturity and confidence mean she is ready to try climbing them.
14 months	By this age most children are up on their feet, though some are steadier than others. If yours isn't walking yet, don't worry – there is still plenty of time to master this skill.
15 months	Control over her chest, head, and legs enables her to take part in a wider range of exploratory play, without needing anyone to help her retain a steady position.

From 8 to 15 Months

What to Do

Hold your baby firmly under her arms, facing you. Gradually lower her toward a solid surface while smiling at her all the time. When her feet touch the floor, she will take her weight on her outstretched legs and might even bounce up and down.

While on the floor facedown, she will make very vigorous attempts to reach an object that attracts her attention. She will probably draw both knees up toward her tummy and her arms will stretch out. With luck, she might move toward the object.

Bring your infant to the standing position by lifting her under her arms, and help her grip the edge of a low table. If you move your hands a couple of inches away from her, she may continue to stand, using the table as support.

Put an object a few feet away from your infant and watch her move along the floor, perhaps by the traditional crawling method of using her hands and knees to get around or the bottom-shuffling method. Either way, she's on the move.

Take your child's hands in yours while she stands facing you. Once she is in a stable standing position, gently move a step backward while coaxing her to move toward you. She might take one or two hesitant steps forward.

Encourage your child to attempt to climb the stairs. However, you will need to be prepared to help her. She'll discover that going down is not as easy as she had expected, and she may burst into tears once she realizes she is stuck halfway.

Stand a few feet away from your child and hold out a toy toward her. When she toddles toward you, go to another part of the room. She will be able to stop, check herself, have a good look at you, and then change direction without falling over.

Your toddler probably has a low child-sized table and chairs that are perfectly suited to her small stature.
Set some small toys on the table for her to play with, and you'll find that she is able to kneel steadily on the chair so that she can grab hold of the toys.

Stimulating Movement: Birth to 3 Months

Although your young baby has an inborn need to explore his surroundings, control over his body movement during these early months is extremely limited. At birth, for instance, he cannot hold his head without support and he can't roll from his back to his side or tummy. That doesn't stop him from trying, however. You'll see many instances of your new baby straining unsuccessfully to move himself into a new position.

As he nears the age of 3 months, however, he spends much more time with the back of his head flat against the crib surface. This increased control lets him have more choice about where he can look. The strength of these early reflexes diminishes, and learned movement takes over.

Suitable Suggestions

The most relaxed position for your young baby when lying in his crib is to be on his back. This provides constant opportunities for him to move his legs in the air and to flap his arms freely. In time, these limb movements will become stronger and more coordinated, but for the moment he needs

Below: Babies love being propped up, but ensure that there is adequate support for head, neck, and back.

time to be allowed to lie on the mattress without being weighed down by heavy crib blankets. As long as the room is comfortable and he is warmly dressed he will enjoy these unconstrained movements.

Of course, if his surroundings stimulate his interest, he will make more of an effort to move from a static position. That's why you should place toys within his line of vision so that he will be encouraged to shift himself

toward them. Even a crib mobile hanging directly above him acts as an incentive to move. Babies are easily bored, so do your best to vary the play items in his crib – a change of scenery keeps his interest strong. His neck muscles are under-developed, that means that he doesn't have much control over his head and chest movements, but he will manage somehow to move in order to see attractive toys.

In addition lying on his back, your baby likes to be placed facedown on the mattress or on a clean floor. When he is in this position, his natural inquisitiveness makes him want to lift his head up. Until

✦✦✦✦✦✦ Top·Tips ✦✦✦✦✦✦✦

1. Let him kick as much as he wants when you change his diaper. He revels in the sense of freedom from constraint, and may suddenly kick his legs in excitement. Keep him stable on the changing mat while he kicks furiously.

2. Lie on the floor with him. The fact is that he adores you and wants you to be with him whenever possible. When you are close to him, he tries to look at you or to move toward you.

3. For safety reasons, keep a close eye on him if he is not in his crib. You'd be amazed how much a young baby can inch his way from one position to another. Despite his poor coordination, he will somehow manage to move.

4. Place toys on one side of his crib today and then on another side tomorrow. Altering positions in this way encourages your baby to use different body muscles when reaching for them.

5. Gradually reduce the amount of support you give his head when lifting him to an upright position. Use your judgment. You certainly shouldn't let his head lag behind, but neither should you do the job when his muscles can do it.

Above: When a newborn baby is held upright with a foot on a flat surface she will automatically lift her leg and put the other down as if walking. This reflex disappears after about six weeks.

the age of 5 or 6 weeks, he won't be able to do this exercise even for a couple of seconds, but from that time onward his maturing neck muscles allow him to raise his head from the resting position for a moment or two. It's a bit like the way an unfit adult might do push-ups! This is good practice for him. In addition to making his day more stimulating, it's another opportunity to develop those very basic movements.

Once your baby is a few months old, another suitable activity is to hold him upright, although you will need to have a firm grip on him because his back can't take the strain on its own. He loves seeing the world this way, and the moment he is propped up, perhaps as you hold him on your knee, his head and neck movements become much more varied and active.

Q&A

Q Why do my baby's leg and arm movements become more agitated when he is upset?

A This is your baby's way of telling you that he's miserable. He can't express his distress through words, so he uses non-verbal communication to let you know what he is feeling. His tears accompanied by rapid limb movements give you an unmistakable message that he is unhappy.

Q Could I damage his legs by bending and stretching them to strengthen them?

A As long as you do this gently, without causing any discomfort, his leg muscles will probably benefit from this exercise. However, don't force him. If you make the leg movements very soft, and you talk happily to your baby as you do so, then he will probably have a great time.

Toys: plastic blocks, rattles that can be held in a small hand, crib activity center, floor-based multi-gym

Stimulating Movement: 4 to 6 Months

Most of the early reflexes governing movement have gone and your baby now exercises a lot more control over her arms, legs, chest, and head. Probably the most significant change in movement in this period is your growing baby's ability to sit up with a decreasing amount of support. And by the age of 6 months, it's a case of "Look at me – I can do it on my own!"

I CAN ROLL

When your baby is around 4 months old, you'll notice that she turns from one side to the other. One moment she was facing the left, yet a few seconds later she faces the right. This is a remarkable feat of coordination, involving head, neck, chest, hips, arms, and legs. She can change her position without waiting for you, that provides a huge boost to her independence.

Similarly, your growing infant can turn from her back to her tummy completely on her own. In addition to giving her more ways to explore and discover, this demonstration of body strength proves that she is getting ready for sitting up, crawling, and walking.

Suitable Suggestions

The tendency for your infant's head to lag behind the rest of her body disappears gradually, enabling her to experience movement without losing control over her head altogether. This makes her feel more secure and consequently she just loves those games in that you sit her on your knees facing you while you gently bounce her up and down. Of course she totters about and she needs you to keep her from falling over, but she thinks this activity is good fun – she'll chuckle loudly with delight!

Other movement games are suitable, too, such as softly swinging her from side to side while holding her firmly. You'll notice her balance steadily improving between the

Right: Once your baby can sit independently a more varied range of toys and activities is available to him.

Above: Putting a favorite toy just out of reach will encourage your baby to push himself forward.

fourth and sixth month, and her confidence with movement also builds up as a result.

•••••••• Top•Tips ••••••••

1. Tickle her under her arms and along her body. Her little legs and arms will show a flurry of activity when you gently tickle her. Don't overdo it or she will burst out crying with too much excitement.

2. When she is facedown, put her favorite toys just out of her reach. Now that she knows she can move toward them, she will try very hard to reach them. Avoid placing the toys too far away or she will give up trying to get them.

3. Move around the room as you talk to her. When she is in a steady sitting position, talk to her. After a few seconds, gradually walk to the other side of the room so that she turns her head to follow. This enhances her head control and balance.

4. Don't tuck her in too tightly at night. She needs room to move while lying in her crib waiting to go to sleep. Covers should be resting on her, rather than tightly tucked in under the mattress. Like you, she wants freedom to change position.

5. Give her small toys to hold while she sits on your lap. Your child's balance skills will improve even more when she concentrates on another activity at the same time. You'll find that while gripping a toy she can sit without toppling.

Easy exercises to encourage her back, chest, and neck muscles can play a bigger part in her daily activities now, though always be careful not to push against her if she resists. Try this: let your infant lie stretched out on the floor and kneel at her feet so that she can focus on your face without difficulty. Then engage her attention and put your index fingers out toward her hands so that she can grip them; once you feel her hands locked around your fingers, raise them a few inches from the ground.

By the age of 4 or 5 months your baby will probably be able to roll over from her stomach to her back. This is easier than the other way around because she is able to use her arms in a pushing action to start the movement off.

Your infant still needs regular periods of lying facedown. It's only in that position that she can push herself against the floor, strengthening her upper torso. By the time she's 6 months old, she can raise her head, shoulders, and chest off the floor, so that only her hips and legs remain in contact with the surface. And if your beaming face is there to greet her, she tries even harder to achieve this target. Don't forget her leg muscles. She may be able to bear her own weight on her feet if you hold her securely under her arms while she is in the standing position. Practice this with her.

Q Why does my 5-month-old usually keep her legs off the crib mattress whereas before she used to rest them on it?

A This is just the effect of the growth in her leg muscles, and the fact that she's no longer as passive. Keeping her legs in the air like this is more comfortable for her, and she can move around more freely without knocking anything.

Q Should I restrain her when she wriggles around during bathtime?

A Your first priority must always be to keep her safe. But if you hold her steady, you can just let her wriggle and splash about. The sensation of warm water against her legs, coupled with the noise of splashing, excites her. Allow an extra few minutes for her bathing routine so that she has this special time to practice her movement skills.

Toys: baby walker, soft play-mat, soft storybook, soft building blocks, bath toys, cushions, wooden shapes, door bouncer

Stimulating Movement: 7 to 9 Months

Now that your child has gained more control over his upper body movement so that he sits up easily, it is his lower body's turn to become more responsive in this next three months. As the early stages of crawling emerge, and perhaps also his first intentional stepping response, he finds totally new ways of moving himself around the house. This opens up new play opportunities and further sharpens his desire to investigate and explore.

FRUSTRATION

Your infant's ambition outstrips his ability when it comes to movement. In other words, he has lofty aims and is none too pleased when reality takes over and he discovers that he can't reach the soft toy that is a few feet away. Tears of frustration flow freely at this age.

Calm him, reassure him, and be prepared to bring the object of his despair over to him. The next time you hear his moans of frustration, try to settle him before he reaches explosion point. He is less likely to become agitated and give up when you are there with him. You need to find a balance between encouraging him to move toward the source of interest and causing him too much frustration.

Suitable Suggestions

From the age of 6 months onward, help your child to practice the sitting and balancing ability he has already acquired. For instance, when he is in that position, place a wide range of attractive toys around him, some on either side, and some outside his range of reach. If allowed to play on his own, he will grab one toy, then put it down to pick up a different toy on his other side. Each time he reaches, grabs, places, turns, and stretches, your infant improves his upper body movements as well as his balance.

It's in this phase that crawling begins. Bear in mind that there are several stages in the development of crawling – he doesn't go from having no crawling skills one day to confidently crawling the next. In fact, one psychological study confirmed that your child has to go through up to 14 different progressions before he can crawl competently! This means he needs encouragement and practice.

Don't be impatient with him because, say, he doesn't yet lift his tummy off the floor when crawling; his crawling movements are simply not mature enough yet. He will improve his crawling ability spontaneously, and there are no specific exercises you should do to hurry the process along. However, make sure he has plenty of opportunities to lie facedown on the floor so that he can use his crawling ability and extend it through practice. You will also find that around the seventh month your baby is competent at rolling from his back to his tummy, as well as the other way

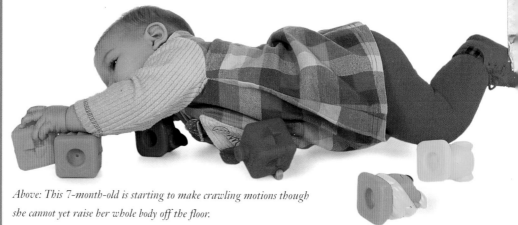

Above: This 7-month-old is starting to make crawling motions though she cannot yet raise her whole body off the floor.

around. This makes life much more interesting for him!

Although your 9-month-old won't have achieved the ability to walk on his own, he will probably have the physical skills and the self-confidence to support himself once he stands up. Every day, put your child in a standing position a couple of times and let him take his own weight by gripping on to a low table or solid, heavy chair that won't topple over.

Bear in mind that he will probably fall over if he lets go, so try not to distract

Above: Supporting your child standing up helps build up the muscle strength and balance she needs for walking.

his attention while he stands. Be ready to catch him should he accidentally lose his grip and balance, reassure him, and then return him to the previous position. Give him lots of cuddles and praise when he manages this particular challenge.

Below: At 9 months this little girl is a confident crawler.

✦✦✦✦✦✦ Top ✦ Tips ✦✦✦✦✦✦

1. Allow him time in the baby walker. He will be happy to sit in a baby walker, although he may not be able to propel it in the desired direction at this stage. If he appears to lean too far over to one side, sit him back in the center once again.

2. Tickle his bare feet. The soles of his feet are very sensitive to a tickling touch. Keep your hand still as you tickle him, so that he can choose whether to draw his legs away or to keep them in that position.

3. Give him simple directions or questions. For instance, when he is sitting surrounded by his toys, ask him "Where is your teddy bear?" He may turn around to look for it, and try to reach it.

4. Play "facing" games. Sit on the floor facing your baby and pass toys to him. Once he is into the rhythm of this passing game, hold the toy a few inches from the normal passing point so that he must lean his body and arms to get it.

5. "Accidentally" drop toys. A good way of encouraging him to use his full chest and hip control is to act as though you intend to hand him a toy but then deliberately let it slip from your grasp. Let him pick it up from where it has fallen.

Q & A

Q My baby is 9 months old. I'm worried he'll hurt himself one of these days when he tries to pull himself up. How can I keep him safe?

A The only way he can learn new movement skills is by tackling new challenges and there is always a minor risk of injury in that situation. Instead of restricting his movements, stay close to him when he maneuvers – that way you are better placed to prevent a potential accident.

Q While other infants seem energetic and active throughout the day, mine just sits there most of the time. Is there something wrong with him?

A His lack of activity probably has more to do with his personality than lack of ability. As long as he is interested in toys and is alert when you talk to him, you have nothing to worry about. He'll probably be one of those children who go from sitting to walking, without the crawling stage in between.

Toys: rattles that are easy to grip, floor-based activity center, soft ball, small toy on wheels, solid ride-on toy

Stimulating Movement: 10 to 12 Months

It's as though your baby's improved balance and body movements, coupled with her increased chest, hips, and leg strength, have all been aiming toward this last section of the first year, because it is in this phase that she might actually take her first independent steps. And even if she hasn't started walking by the age of 12 months, she will almost certainly be well on the way to that achievement.

Suitable Suggestions

Your child's crawling skills remain important and you should continue to encourage them in new ways. For instance, you can put your child in one corner of the room and then attract her attention when you are in the opposite corner. This is good exercise for her, and she likes the experience of moving over relatively longer distances. You can also build mini obstacle courses for her to negotiate – a thick cushion placed strategically between you and her means she has to climb over it to reach you. If her motivation is high enough, she'll cross that hurdle without too much effort.

Right: At about a year your child is likely to be supporting herself with one hand and cruising the furniture.

Do your best to get her to move while on her feet. One way is to help her to a standing position (or let her get there herself) and hold her hands firmly in yours so that she can't fall backward, forward, or

Left: You can help your child to take her first steps by holding her hands and giving lots of verbal encouragement.

sideways. As she watches you slowly edge backward away from her, she may try to take a step forward. If she stays rooted to the spot, give her lots of verbal encouragement to come toward you; you can even gently pull at her hands to indicate the direction in that she needs to move.

Another way is to let her rest in the standing position while holding on to a long range of furniture for support. This gives her the confidence to sidestep her way along. For instance, you could place her at one end of a long sofa and wait at the other end for her. Or you could put a series of small chairs in a

Above: Most children love to be swung, but always support them under the arms; never swing them by the arms.

row so that she can edge her way along from one end to the other without having to sit down in between.

Remember that the act of walking requires not only good balance and body movements but also lots of confidence. Often it is this lack of self-belief that keeps a child from taking her first independent step – she is afraid of falling over. That's why she needs you to be patient and supportive. Do everything you can to relax and encourage her to walk, but don't make her anxious about it or else she will prefer to remain in the safe stage of sitting.

Below: Babies often first pull themselves to a standing position using the bars of the crib or playpen.

Top·Tips

1. Use her playpen as a support frame. If she is inside her playpen as you approach, lean over the top and put your hands part of the way down toward her. Wait until she pulls herself to standing using the pen bars before taking her hands in yours.

2. Make movement games fun. Of course you want your 1-year-old to walk. Getting irritated with her won't help and will only make her grumpy; this reduces her confidence and makes her reluctant to try. Keep it fun.

3. Allow success. There's no point in asking too much of your child. She needs to achieve success in challenges involving movement or her enthusiasm will diminish. When she does achieve at a new level, let her know you are delighted.

4. Steadily increase the spaces between the furniture. Once she starts to cruise around the room using the furniture for support, gradually extend the gaps between each item so that she almost has to lunge at the next one.

5. Expect episodes of little progress. There may be periods of development where progress seems to be at a standstill or even goes backward. That happens with many children. Her progress will start again when she is ready and confident.

Q&A

Q Should I let go of her hands suddenly so that she is left standing alone and is compelled to take a step?

A That could in theory motivate your child to walk, though it is more likely to terrify her. Dramatic gestures like that can backfire, making her less willing to trust you next time.

Q Since my toddler fell a couple of times trying to walk, she doesn't try anymore. What should I do?

A Give her time to restore her confidence in her walking skills. You'll find that her natural drive to walk independently will surface again after a few days, once she has recovered from this temporary upset. In the meantime, don't pressure her into walking.

Toys: wooden toddler cart with bricks, large sit-and-ride toy, large wooden cubes for sidestepping, child-sized chair

Stimulating Movement: 13 to 15 Months

The majority of children take their first few walking steps before they reach the age of 15 months (the average age is 13 months). And what a surge of excitement this brings your child. No longer restricted to a particular area, he can launch himself into totally new adventures of discovery. His steadiness while walking rapidly increases and he toddles about the place, totally fearless and full of his own importance.

HE'S STILL NOT WALKING

If your 15-month-old child hasn't taken his first step yet, don't worry. There are some children who don't walk until a few months later and yet whose subsequent development proves to be perfectly normal. It's just that their genetic blueprint has pre-programmed walking to occur at a later time than usual.

What matters is that the other positive signs of movement progress are there, such as he tries to crawl, he kicks his legs when lying in his crib, he pulls himself to standing, and he reaches out for toys. If these positive features are present, you can be sure he'll walk very soon. If you are concerned, talk to your pediatrician, who can reassure you.

Suitable Suggestions

The most important help you can give your child at this stage is to increase his confidence and stability when walking. Despite his determination to stand on his own two feet, he may be nervous about being in such an exposed upright position – the world certainly looks different from up there! And all it takes is a minor fall or bump to give him a little setback. That's why he needs lots of praise and encouragement from you when he starts to walk. Be there with him when you can, smiling at him, telling him how terrific he is, and giving him a big cuddle when he manages on his own.

At first, he will probably walk with his arms stretched out on

Right: When your child first learns to walk she will often need to pause to steady herself.

either side, rather like a poorly coordinated tight-rope walker, and his body movements will be very jerky. That's fine; he's just feeling his way very carefully and letting his balance system adjust to the new sensations. Within a month or so you will find that his arms are closer to his side and his forward steps are smoother, less shaky, and altogether more relaxed.

Now that he is a toddler in the true sense of the word, you have to think seriously about keeping him safe without restricting him too much. When you take him shopping with you, for instance, he wants to hurry along the wide, flat aisles of the supermarket. That's a great opportunity for him to practice his movement skills.

But he can move fast, and the last thing you want to happen is for him to lunge for the items on the shelf before you can stop him or even disappear from your sight. You may find a harness helpful (the type that fits around your child's upper body).

This is also the time when he extends his other movement skills, such as climbing. When he approaches stairs, he is unlikely to climb them in a standing position. Almost certainly, he still lowers himself to either a

Left: At 15 months this little boy's balance is good enough to allow him to bend down to pick up a toy.

sitting or a kneeling position and ascends the entire flight that way. However, his increased leg strength and coordination allow him to progress upward at a faster rate than before. He needs your supervision when climbing.

Below: Some children are fearless climbers and will try to escape their cribs at a surprisingly early age.

✦✦✦✦✦✦✦ Top ✦ Tips ✦✦✦✦✦✦✦

1. Comfort him when he falls. His unstable walking position renders him vulnerable to falls, and this can upset your toddler. Comfort him, cuddle him, and get him back on his feet right away. He'll soon forget his moment of distress.

2. Let him climb in and out of his chair without help. This is a very complex challenge, but is one he can master given enough time. The twisting, kneeling, and turning involved provides excellent practice for his balance and movement skills.

3. Ask him to pick up toys from the floor. When toddling about, your child will be willing to lift a toy from the floor. He stops beside it, slowly bends his knees with his bottom pushed right back, then picks it up. He improves with practice.

4. Play kicking games with him. He will not be able to stand still and kick the ball very well – the chances are that he will miss or fall backward, or both! Yet he enjoys trying this new play opportunity.

5. Give him space. Your toddler is a dynamic explorer, and he doesn't need much encouragement to go wherever his curiosity takes him. Make sure he also has lots of time to develop his walking and balance skills spontaneously, without direction.

Q Is it normal for a toddler to walk a bit, then crawl, then walk another bit, then crawl?

A Yes. A child rarely abandons his earlier mode of travel as soon as he learns to walk. After all, he knows that crawling is a very efficient and rapid form of movement that isn't tiring. Walking, however, is slower and more exhausting to start with. That's why he still uses crawling to cover longer distances.

Q Should my toddler wear shoes inside the house as well as when he is outside?

A The main purpose of shoes is to provide protection for his feet, not to give him better balance. At this stage, therefore, he should still be allowed to walk around carpeted areas in bare feet so that his toes and foot muscles are fully exercised.

🧸🚚 **Toys:** pull-along toy, sit-and-ride toy, small and large soft ball, child-sized table and chair, inflatable wading pool.

Hand-Eye

Coordination

The Importance of Hand–Eye Coordination

The world is a fascinating place for your young baby. There is so much she wants to learn, so many things she wants to discover – and between birth and 15 months, her main means of exploring is through looking and touching.

Right from birth, she spends time watching the world around her, sometimes just taking in the information she sees, sometimes reaching out to get directly involved, and often combining both vision and touch. It is this process of hand–eye coordination (that involves many aspects, such as focusing, looking, reaching, touching, grabbing, lifting, and throwing) that occupies so much of her time.

That's why you'll find she constantly reaches out for any object that is within range. To you, that small cardboard box is a boring bit of old trash just waiting to be thrown out, but to your young, curious baby it's an exciting treasure just waiting to be explored by her eager little fingers – she wants to know how to get the lid off in order to see what lies inside. Likewise, you know that an electric socket

Left: Most of your newborn baby's movements are instinctive, not deliberate.

must be avoided by little fingers at all costs, whereas your baby can't believe her luck when she finds such a treasure chest within her reach.

Your infant's ability to control her hands and fingers – and to watch these movements closely – allows her to explore, to discover, and to learn about the world around her. For instance, using hand–eye coordination, she tries to pull the rattle close to her face so that she can peer closely at it, shake it, and even put it in her mouth! Early hand–eye coordination boosts her progress with learning.

Reflexes

As you will have already discovered, however, your baby appears to have virtually no control over her hand movements at birth and for several weeks after. It's as though her hands have a will of their own; you may find, for instance, that during feeding one of her hands suddenly arrives from nowhere and hits against you! Rest assured, she is not doing that deliberately.

The fact is that your baby's early vision and touch skills are dominated by a number of reflexes

with which she was born. These are physical reactions over which she has no control and that happen automatically without your baby thinking about them at all. It is instinctive behavior. Many reflexes are connected with survival (such as the sucking reflex, which causes your baby to suck whenever a nipple is placed in her mouth). Some early reflexes, however, are connected with hand–eye coordination. These include

• **blinking.** If your baby hears a sudden loud noise, or if an object approaches her face very quickly, her eyes automatically close. This is a very primitive form of self-protection that is present at birth and lasts throughout life. At the end of the first year, for instance, she'll still blink when a toy slips from her grasp and crashes to the floor.

• **palmar grasp.** When your young baby is lying on her back with her

Below: Once your child is on the move, keep anything hazardous well out of reach.

Above: A 7-month-old baby is able to target an object, pick it up, and move it, very often to her mouth.

hands in the air, gently place your index finger in the palm of her hand so that she can feel the pressure of your touch. Her hands will automatically grasp your finger very tightly, and she will seem unable to let go. This reflex is present at birth but usually disappears by the time she is 3 or 4 months old.

• **Moro reflex.** Be very gentle when testing this reflex. Hold your baby firmly in your hands so that she faces you. Then quickly lower her 6 inches (while still gripping her securely). The Moro reflex (also known as the startle reflex) forces her to arch her back and to throw her arms and legs into the air, as though she is trying to grab on to something. This vanishes by the age of 4 months.

Action Without Understanding

At the same time as your infant grows out of these early primitive reflexes, her hand–eye coordination develops in a more structured way. But remember that she doesn't yet understand the implications of her actions. That's why, for instance, she happily grabs the glasses

Right: By 15 months or so toddlers can exert good control over simple tools such as a hammer.

from your face and cheerfully twists them till they fall apart. It's genuine curiosity that drives her behavior, nothing else.

So try not to get annoyed with her when you realize your 6-month-old has scrunched up the letter you received earlier that morning, and then happily drenched it in saliva as she tried to chew it. Of course, you have to set limits on her behavior or else within a few months your home will be totally chaotic, but do your best to achieve this without losing your temper at her explorations using vision and touch. If you do become continually angry with her for this sort of behavior, you run the risk of making your baby afraid to reach out and investigate.

The same caution applies to safety. Exploration is the name of the game when it comes to

hand–eye coordination during your baby's first year. Small beads are things to be picked up, chewed, and swallowed, as far as she is concerned. Concerns about choking, vomiting, or eating dirt don't bother your inquisitive baby at all. Her determination to discover is the only impulse she responds to, and hand–eye coordination enables her to interact with her surroundings. Simply keep an eye on her to make sure she remains safe.

Hand–Eye Coordination

Age	Skill
1 week	Your baby is born with many reflex involuntary actions that he can't control, one of which is his grasping response.
1 month	He starts to watch objects that are close to his face and that also move slowly from one side to the other.
2 months	Hand control begins at this age as his fingers become more flexible. He peers with interest at his fingers.
3 months	He watches an object as it slowly moves within his line of sight, and if he thinks it is close enough, he will stretch out his hand toward it.
4 months	His understanding has increased so that he can now anticipate routine events and reach out as though to hurry them along.
5 months	Hand–eye coordination improves to the point where he starts to look for an object that slips from his grasp.
6 months	His hand and finger movements are more coordinated now, and he begins to use both hands in synchrony.
7 months	He is able to play with toys more purposefully and explores them in new and interesting ways.

From Birth to 7 Months

What to Do

Hold your baby firmly in your left arm, and place the index finger of your right hand into the palm of his hand. He will automatically grip his hand tightly around your finger; pull it away and you'll find he won't let go.

Move your face close to his and give him a big smile. As he stares at you closely, whether he laughs or not, softly move your head a few inches to one side and then a few inches to the other. He will follow you intently as your head moves.

Let him see you place a small object gently in the palm of his hand. Within a few seconds his little fingers will close tightly around it, and he may move his hand as if trying to bring the object to his face.

Place a hanging mobile above his crib, but just outside his reach. Blow gently to activate the dangling items. Very soon the movement of the mobile will catch his attention, and he will reach out to grasp the different sections dangling above him.

Whether you breast-feed or bottle-feed your baby, place him in a position so that he can see you prepare for the feeding. You'll notice that he becomes very excited and pushes his hands and arms toward the food source long before it is within range.

Reach out to give your baby a small toy. Just as his hands start to touch the toy, let it drop from your hand so that it falls on the floor. Look puzzled, then ask him in a clear voice, "Where is the toy?" He may look down toward the floor for it.

Take two small wooden cubes. Pass one of them to your baby and let him hold it firmly in his hand. Quickly but gently place the second block in his other hand. He can probably hold them both simultaneously for a very short time before letting go.

Provide your infant with a wide range of toys. Instead of simply putting them in his mouth, he will shake them, rattle them, and even bang them together to make a noise. If you make a big fuss over him when he does this, he'll continue to play with them.

Hand–Eye Coordination

Age	Skill
8 months	Your baby can coordinate his thumb and index finger, using them together in a pincerlike movement.
9 months	Hand movements are more within his control, and he can coordinate them much more efficiently now.
10 months	He loves playing with toys that can move across the floor, even though he still cannot walk independently.
11 months	He is fascinated by containers and is very determined to explore them with his hands in order to find whatever is inside them.
1 year	His hand–eye coordination and understanding have increased to the point where he can use toys constructively in play.
13 months	He can use his hand to indicate to you that he wants a particular object; he may try to speak to you at the same time.
14 months	Your child starts to show that he knows how to use pencils and crayons appropriately, rather than simply putting them straight into his mouth.
15 months	His hand control has extended significantly now, and he is probably able to hold two items in each hand at the same time.

From 8 to 15 Months

What to Do

Sit your baby in his high chair and then place small portions of finger food in the tray in front of him. He will reach out, controlling his index finger and thumb to lift the pieces up to his mouth.

Take a piece of string and tie one end around a small toy. Having attracted your infant's attention to it, demonstrate how you can get the toy to come toward you by pulling the string. Then give him the string and watch to see if he copies you.

Sit on the floor and position your child so that he sits on the floor facing you. Take a small soft ball and roll it slowly toward him. He will stop it in his hand, pick it up, and might even try to roll it back toward you.

Take an empty cardboard box with a lid and place a couple of small toys or wooden blocks inside. Show the closed box to your child, shake it in front of him, then pass the box to him. His curiosity will force him to pry the lid off to see the contents.

When your infant is settled on the floor, give him a plastic cup, a plastic saucer, and a plastic spoon to hold. He will play with these toys appropriately, perhaps putting the cup on top of the saucer or putting the spoon into the cup.

Once your toddler has completed his meal (but while still seated firmly in his high chair), place his favorite toy on a table beside his tray. Make sure this toy catches his attention but is out of his reach. He will probably use his index finger to point to it.

Place a small, chubby crayon in his hand and put a thick, solid pad of paper beside him. Then demonstrate how rubbing the crayon against the paper in any direction creates a mark. You'll see that he tries to make a mark on the paper, too.

Place your child in a comfortable but upright sitting position, with his back straight. Take a couple of quite small toys and put them in his left hand. Immediately put another two in his right hand. He'll hold all four in his hands for a few seconds.

Stimulating Hand–Eye Coordination: Birth to 3 Months

Your young baby needs lots of time to watch what is going on around her. Her head moves from side to side as she lies in her crib, captivated by everything she sees, and she desperately wants to reach out and touch, even though her hand–eye coordination has barely started at this stage. Her innate need to discover and learn new things forces her to interact with her surroundings.

GRAB HER ATTENTION

To stimulate your baby's interest, place a hanging mobile above her crib. Position it so that it is well out of her reach (or else you can be assured she'll grab it) yet close enough to be within her vision (just above the highest point of the crib). If you choose a mobile that also makes a noise when activated, so much the better.

Let your baby watch you doing routine household chores. Filling and emptying the washing machine is a boring household task for most people. However, your young baby loves to watch you moving around the house like that. If possible, position her in such a way that she can see you easily.

Suitable Suggestions

During these first three months, your baby is very dependent on you to bring toys to her. Without your help and support, she'll soon become bored lying in her crib or carriage because she isn't yet able

Right: Introduce your baby to toys with stimulating textures and colors when she is calm and alert.

to reach out in a coordinated manner. So be prepared literally to put toys into her hands until she grabs hold of them. And once she has the toy within her grasp, gently move her arm to and fro. The more you demonstrate these activities to her, and help her carry them out, the more likely she is to repeat them herself.

Brightly colored, noisy toys are the most suitable type during this period; babies find it easier to distinguish primary colors (red, yellow, blue) than combined colors (such as purple, green, orange). Their sights and sounds attract her attention, making her want to discover all she can about them. And don't forget to use picture books. Sure, she can't turn the pages or tell you the names of the objects shown in the pictures, but she will stare at them and try to touch them; because your baby doesn't realize the difference between a picture and the real thing, she tries to feel the objects displayed on the pages.

Q Is it safe for me leave some toys in the crib so that she can play with them whenever she wants?

A As long as you are sure the items are safe for young children and do not need to be kept under adult supervision, it's fine to leave some toys at the side of the crib. Apart from staring at them, she will also reach for them. It's good to give her this sort of independence early on.

Q Should we choose curtains with patterns for our baby?

A Yes. You want your baby's bedroom to look attractive, and child-centered patterns on curtains (such as brightly colored cartoon characters set against a white or light background) are great for your baby, too. She spends lots of time looking at her immediate environment, and attractive colors and patterns will encourage her interest.

Change your baby's play position when possible. Interestingly, the same toy will have a different appeal for her when she lies flat, compared with its appeal when she is upright. For instance, your baby will smile happily when you hold her in your arms and show her a rattle, even though she showed

Above: A young baby will be fixated by a colorful hanging mobile.

no interest in the same toy a few minutes before while lying in her crib.

Babies love a gentle tug-of-war over a toy, as long as they win! Dangle, say, a child's plastic ring above her until she grabs hold of it firmly. Then softly pull at the other side, while smiling at her. You'll notice her grip strengthen, and you can let the ring be rocked backward and forward in this mock tugging situation. Be warned, however: if by mistake you pull so hard that she lets the ring slip from her fingers, she'll almost certainly be furious and will burst into tears.

Below: Baby gyms provide lots of visual interest initially and your baby will find it very exciting once he can make the toys move.

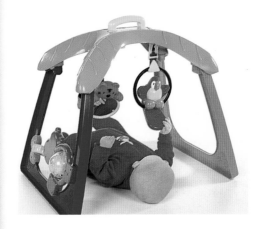

✧✧✧✧✧✧✧ Top · Tips ✧✧✧✧✧✧✧

1. Buy her toys that can be gripped easily by small hands. Large toys are too difficult for her to hold and she will lose interest in them. She likes to grasp objects and then bring them close to her face so that she can peer closely at them.

2. By all means place a toy so that she has to make an effort to reach it. If you see that she struggles in vain, however, give it to her eventually; if you don't, she may lose interest and give up.

3. Provide her with a variety of toys, if possible. Although all rattles, for example, might seem the same to you, each one is special to your baby and she sees different qualities in them.

4. Be prepared to demonstrate hand movements to your baby if you see that she plays repetitively. This gives her an example of novel hand movements, which she may try to copy.

5. Assuming you buy her toys that are safe for young children, let your baby put them into her mouth to explore their properties. This is another dimension of hand–eye coordination.

Stimulating Hand–Eye Coordination: 4 to 6 Months

Your baby changes dramatically throughout this period. He is altogether more reactive to you and to his general surroundings. With more purpose behind his vision and touch, your infant becomes an active explorer, using his hand–eye coordination in a more focused and controlled way. This shift toward a greater level of control helps him become more actively involved.

SET LIMITS

He's still quite young but you could consider setting up some rules about touching. Make a point of warning him about small items. Your baby still likes to put things in his mouth, although he is more aware of the dangers this poses. When you see him about to put a small item in his mouth, firmly but quietly say "no" and remove the object from his hand. You will have to repeat this process again and again and again.

Set some "no go" areas in your home. Decide what objects you don't want him to explore (for instance, your china knickknacks, electric sockets, electrical items) and tell him not to touch these. Of course he will forget and touch them anyway. You need to keep reminding him.

Suitable Suggestions

If he drops a toy you'll notice that he actively searches for it with his eyes, and if he pinpoints it with his vision, he'll do everything he can to grab hold of it. Encourage him to look for objects that are not immediately at hand but are within his visual range. Your question "Where's the ball?" prods him into action. He loves your attention and interest.

Below: In the early months all babies use their mouths as well as their hands to explore objects.

Use everyday opportunities as they arise naturally. Whatever you are doing while he is with you, talk to your growing child. He likes to watch you move around the room, and even if his attention is momentarily distracted, he quickly turns back to you when you start to talk to him again.

Bathtime is a great opportunity for letting your baby use his hands to splash the water. At first, he may give himself a fright; if the water sprays into his face he'll blink furiously and might even burst out crying,

but settle him, reassure him, and calm him down. Soapy bubbles have a lovely texture, though make sure he doesn't rub any into his eyes. As long as you are relaxed while bathing him, he will thoroughly enjoy this special time of the day.

✦✦✦✦✦✦✦ Top·Tips ✦✦✦✦✦✦✦

1. Show enthusiasm for his explorations. He wants to please you at every opportunity, so give him a big smile when you see him reaching, touching, and exploring to heighten his enjoyment and enthusiasm for this activity.

2. Keep safety in mind at all times. Aside from the obvious worry about your child hurting himself, the reality is that injury or discomfort resulting from him touching or swallowing something will dampen his enthusiasm for exploring.

3. Show him how to pass from one hand to the other. Easy for you but difficult for your infant, passing a small toy from his left to right hand (or vice versa) is a skill he might achieve, especially if you demonstrate this to him.

4. Laugh when he makes a noise with rattles. Sit with him while he bangs them hard against the side of the crib or on the floor. When he sees that you are not at all upset by the noise, he will be happy to continue playing this way.

5. Let him reach for picture books. When he snuggles up to you while you talk to him about the pictures in his book, allow him to grab hold of the thick cardboard pages if he wants to have a closer look by himself.

Left: Big cloth books are an ideal way of introducing your baby to the idea of turning pages.

His increasing general physical maturity also helps to develop his hand–eye coordination. For instance, toward the sixth month your infant can sit up on the floor while supported either by you or by strategically placed cushions. This changes his entire perspective and makes life more interesting for him. The typical child of this age loves to sit upright, legs splayed, while picking up and dropping toys from his hands to the floor.

If your infant tries to grab hold of the bottle or the spoon while having his meal, let him (though don't let go yourself). Food is a great incentive for him to extend his hand–eye coordination skills! True, he's likely to make a terrible mess at this stage, but that's all part of child development. You may decide sometimes to give finger food as a snack, and this helps, too.

Below: At 6 months your baby will still put most things to his mouth – this can be a good time to introduce finger foods.

Q&A

Q Should I move knick-knacks out of the way of my 5-month-old baby or is that just giving in to him?

A. It's best to remove possible temptations. Like it or not, you may have to change the way your household is organized in order to accommodate the increasing hand–eye coordination skills of your infant. It's far easier to remove a fragile knickknack altogether than to worry constantly that he'll get his hands on it.

Q What other strategies can I use to keep him safe?

A. Praise him when he follows the rules. There is no bigger incentive for your baby to stick to rules about touching than your approval. He'll beam with delight when you cuddle him for not going near that hot radiator, and he'll feel very self-satisfied when you hug him for staying away from the electric socket.

Toys: baby walker, soft play-mat, soft storybook, soft building blocks, bath toys, cushions, wooden shapes, door bouncer

Stimulating Hand–Eye Coordination: 7 to 9 Months

Now that your baby's ability to sit on her own is well established and she can make a good attempt to propel herself along the floor by crawling, there's no stopping her. She will do just about anything to get hold of that toy, even if it is under a chair or on top of a shelf. She has no fear of danger; all that matters to her is the enticing prospect of reaching the object of her desire.

SHE GIVES UP TOO EASILY

You may not discover that your infant gives up easily until she turns to you one day in tears, distressed by her inability to stack the rings on the central pillar or to bring the food to her mouth the way she had intended.

If you think your child gives up too easily, give her gentle encouragement to complete the task, but don't force her. And make a point of setting a good example yourself. Let her see you struggle with a similar task while still smiling (for instance, pouring water from a jug to a cup). This will persuade her to adopt a similar attitude.

Suitable Suggestions

There is a wide range of suitable activities for stimulating hand–eye coordination now. For instance, you can encourage your baby's pincer grasp. As she has better control over her hand movements, she can use her thumb and forefinger together in a pincer grip rather like a pair of pliers. Of course, a small object can easily slip from between her fingers, but this skill improves with practice.

Above: Stacking rings are an excellent toy for helping your child improve her coordination.

You can use small bits of food, or small toy blocks (though keep a close eye on her in case she tries to swallow them). She can do this while sitting in her high chair.

Practice action–reaction movements with her. Your child is more aware of the connection

Above: Songs with clapping actions are a great way to teach your child this skill.

between her hand movements and the world around her. You can help develop this skill. For example, sit your child on the floor and place a flat, clean tissue beside her so that one corner is a few inches away from her hand. Then place a small toy in the opposite corner and ask your child to pull the tissue toward you. She may need several shots before she pulls the tissue to get the toy.

You can now have fun playing "musical instruments" with your infant. Find a couple of old pots and pans and add a wooden spoon or two. Then pass this fine orchestral array to your enthusiastic 8-month-old. Before you know it she will be banging the spoon against the pot, the pot against the pan, and the lid against the spoon.

Your child will enjoy filling and emptying cups. Face her and let her see you put a wooden block into a plastic cup, and then turn the cup upside down so that the block falls out. Do this a couple of times, then say "You do this." Hand the cup and block to her and give her lots of prompts to put the block back into the cup. She may have difficulty with this at first, so keep encouraging her until she completes the task successfully.

Below: This little girl is picking up banana pieces with thumb and forefinger in a pincer grip.

✦✦✦✦✦✦✦ Top·Tips ✦✦✦✦✦✦✦

1. Avoid comparisons. Every child is different, and you may find that your friend's child has more advanced hand–eye coordination skills than your child even though they are both the same age. Comparisons will de-motivate her.

2. Use pointing. When the two of you sit together, point to something in the room and say to her "Look at that"; she will follow the line of your hand to the object. Then ask her to point to a specific object in the room.

3. Play with a wind-up car. Try to get one of those toy cars that is powered either by winding it up or by battery. Take your child into a room in the house that does not have a carpet, and then let the car go. She'll watch it run all over the place.

4. Tickle her palms. Basic songs and rhymes that involve tickling her hands (such as "This Llittle Piggy") playfully force her to keep her hand in one position, then hurriedly remove it.

5. Leave toys in her crib. Your infant almost certainly wakes up earlier in the morning than you would like. That's why it's good to leave a pile of toys within reach so that she can play on her own without needing your attention.

Q&A

Q My baby is 8 months old and gets angry when she can't complete a puzzle toy. What should I do?

A React calmly to her frustration. When she simply can't manage that hand–eye coordination activity and consequently erupts with fury, don't let yourself get riled. Do your best to soothe her, then suggest she try again. If she still doesn't succeed, put the item away and come back to it again later.

Q Is there any point in expecting my infant to play quietly? She really likes to make a loud noise.

A Naturally you don't want to discourage her from playing, but now is as good a time as any to teach her that there are other people to consider. When she makes a particularly loud noise, speak quietly to her and ask her to be more gentle. She'll respond to you, at least for a few seconds.

Stimulating Hand–Eye Coordination: 10 to 12 Months

As he approaches the final quarter of his first year, your baby's self-confidence has vastly improved. Progress in all areas of his development including hand–eye coordination means he is a more independent and determined child. He likes to make his own amusement and isn't too happy when you tell him what he can and can't do. On the other hand, he remains desperate for your love and approval and doesn't like you to be angry with him.

WHEN HE'S PASSIVE

Children differ in their level of desire to explore; some are more dynamic than others. If yours is one of those who won't reach out for toys and isn't very eager to explore, then be prepared to bring toys to him, place them gently in his hands, and play with him. This will increase his motivation. He needs you to push him gently into more activities.

Also, be sure that he has toys suitable for his stage of development. If he has only toys suitable for a much older or much younger child, then he is unlikely to show much interest in them.

Left: Once your child can put a lid on a box, this new skill will keep her occupied and give her tremendous satisfaction.

Below: Allowing a child to feed himself will help his coordination and make him more interested in his food.

Suitable Suggestions

Boxes with lids fascinate your child now. They don't need to be fancy or expensive to arouse his curiosity. All you need to do is take a small cardboard box with a reasonably tight-fitting lid, place a small object inside it, then put the lid back on. Bring the box over to your toddler and shake it backward and forward so that the object rattles around noisily. After a couple of seconds, hand the box to him without saying a word. He will immediately try to remove the lid to discover what's inside. Having achieved that, he will be content to spend a few minutes trying to fit the lid back onto the box.

His advanced hand–eye coordination means that he can attempt more complex tasks, such as ordering shapes of different sizes. He enjoys the challenge of nesting cubes, a series of boxes of diminishing size that fit neatly inside one another when placed in a specific order. Your child will find this hard

to complete. However, he will rise to the demands of this toy and will be pleased to show you that at least two or three of the boxes fit inside each other.

Left: At around this age your child may be ready to start some supervised scribbling with chalk or crayons.

He loves sitting in the bath at the end of the day, playing with his toy water containers. Assuming he feels confident sitting in the bath (with you beside him), give him some plastic cups or jugs and suggest that he pour water from one container into another. This can turn out to be a particularly messy game but it's great for improving his hand control. He can pour from the left hand to the right, or the other way around. Encourage him to pour slowly and to take his time.

Your child's increased use and grasp of spoken language means that you can give him direct commands involving hand–eye coordination. For instance, tell him gently, "Give me the cup"; he should be able to look around to see where the cup is, pick it up in his hand, and then pass it to you. You'll see him concentrate very hard during this activity as he uses all his concentration to get it right.

Below: By this age your child is more likely to have the patience and dexterity to build a small tower of stacking cups or blocks.

✦✦✦✦✦✦✦ Top · Tips ✦✦✦✦✦✦✦

1. Play lots of hand games with him. He enjoys action rhymes involving hand movements, such as "Itsy Bitsy Spider," or games like "Pat-a-Cake." These games are great fun and also involve hand–eye coordination.

2. Get him involved in feeding. When you have a bit more time than usual, give your child the spoon to hold. He will make a good effort to bring the spoon to his mouth, though much of the food will already have fallen off.

3. Provide varied textures. If you can face the prospect of cleaning up a mess, give your toddler bowls containing different textures such as custard, water and flour, and dried oats. Let him put his hands into each bowl to feel the different textures.

4. Offer solutions. If you see that he is stuck at a particular hand–eye coordination puzzle (for instance, putting a shape into the shape-sorter) suggest other ways he could try to do this. Stay with him as he tries out these suggestions.

5. Continue to support him. Despite his increased independence, he still has more fun playing when you are involved. By all means step back a little and give him space to explore on his own, but do remember he still needs you.

Q Now that my child is very steady when sitting, is it safe to leave him playing alone in a shallow bath while I prepare a meal for his older brother?

A No. It is never safe to leave a child of this age alone in bathwater. He could slip in a split second and be submerged in only a few inches of water. Far better for your older child to wait until his brother's bathtime is finished than to take such a risk.

Q No matter how often I show my toddler how to put the shapes in his shape-sorter toy, he still can't manage them all. Should he be able to?

A Shape-sorters are incredibly difficult for little fingers to manage. Your son probably manages the circle and square shapes but not the more complicated ones. Give him time to learn the solutions. As his hand control increases over the next few months, he will fit more shapes into the right holes.

🧸🚚 **Toys:** nesting cups, stacking cubes, shape-sorters, chunky crayons and some paper, musical wind-up toy, bouncer

Stimulating Hand–Eye Coordination: 13 to 15 Months

Your toddler's drive toward independence now increases. Her increased hand–eye coordination skills mean that she has much more control over her environment; they allow her to manipulate toys and other objects in any way she wants, and she can play with a wider range of toys that are more challenging. You may find that her frustration increases and that she becomes angry with herself if, for instance, the building blocks won't lock together in the way she would like them to.

Left: Once past a year toddlers will be absorbed by toys that come apart and can be put together again.

Suitable Suggestions

Your child is especially fascinated by puzzles that draw on her increased learning skills and her hand–eye coordination. Give her a small wooden inset board, the type that has a piece cut out in a circle shape, for example. Your child has to fit the missing piece back into its empty space on the board. She will enjoy trying these puzzles, though do remember that they are extremely difficult for her. Elementary shapes such as circles and squares are the best ones to go for. Your toddler may spend lots of time sitting in silence with an intense expression on her face as she tries to complete the puzzle. If you find that she almost gets the shape in the right place but can't quite manage it, give the piece a gentle nudge until it drops into the hole.

It's important not to de-motivate your child at this stage. Buy her inset-board puzzles that have only one or two pieces in them. She can't deal with more complex puzzles, and they may be so difficult that they discourage her altogether.

The typical child of this age is also fascinated by building towers of things, usually of blocks. Until now, any attempts by her to place one block on top of another would probably have resulted in total failure; her immature hand–eye coordination skills would have meant that she couldn't balance the top block properly. At this stage in her development, though, chances are that she can build a tower of two or even three blocks without it falling over. But she needs your encouragement. Practice this with her

Above: Copying real-life activities like using the telephone is great fun, and of course the actual thing is far better than a toy.

Left: Encourage your child to start to do things for himself. He will enjoy contributing to the dressing – and undressing – process.

❖❖❖❖❖❖❖ Top ❖ Tips ❖❖❖❖❖❖❖

1. Give her plenty of time to complete tasks involving hand control. Your child can't, for instance, pull her sweater on very quickly. So if you want her to achieve this target, avoid a time when you are in a rush.

2. Calm her if she becomes frustrated. She will almost certainly aim to master challenges that are much too difficult for her, and she needs you to calm her, to reassure her, and to direct her to activities that are within her abilities.

3. Don't force hand preference. By now she may start to show preference for one hand over the other. Let this aspect of hand control develop naturally. Certainly, you should never force a left-handed child to use her right hand instead.

4. Play rolling the ball with her. Stand 10 or 12 feet back from her and softly roll a small ball toward her. Your child will love this game, either hitting it away when it comes near or trying to stop it and grab it.

5. Give her a toy telephone. She's seen you lift the telephone receiver to your ear often enough and wants to do this with her own phone. A small plastic or wooden toy phone will provide loads of amusement for your child.

regularly and let her look at a tower you have built as an example.

Many children of this age like to get involved with dressing and undressing. For instance, as you approach with her pullover, she may stick her hands and arms toward you in anticipation. That's terrific because she is proving to you that her understanding, vision, and touch have advanced to the point where she can predict your actions and can try to help you with the task. And one day you are bound to discover that she has pulled her socks off and thrown them over to the other side of the room!

Below: Shape-sorters are ideal for this age group, though the more complex shapes may still prove quite a challenge.

Q My child is afraid to play with new toys. What can I do?

A Be patient with her. If you know that she prefers familiar toys to new ones, just place the new toy alongside her other toys without saying anything. Let her explore it in her own time. After a few days, sit with her and handle the new toy yourself without saying anything about it. Your interest will eventually encourage your child to play with it, too.

Q Is it better to give my toddler a large ball or a small ball to play with?

A She will be able to hold a small ball in her hands but will have difficulty trying to throw it. However, a large ball may block her vision when she holds it in preparation for throwing. The best solution is to go for an in-between size, one that she can hold firmly between both hands while still being able to see easily over the top of it.

Language

The Development of Language

Your baby's use of language changes so much during the first 15 months that it's hard for you to notice all the key changes that occur. From a newborn baby whose only method of communication with you is nonverbal because he can't actually make clear sounds, he has become transformed a year later into an active talker who has already spoken his first clear word.

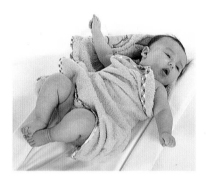

What's even more amazing is that your child develops language in a systematic way. If you've ever tried to learn a foreign language, you'll know what it is like to be confronted with thousands of sounds and millions of words. Well, that's what it is like for your baby; in fact, the challenge for him is even more difficult because he can't draw on any previous experience of learning a language. There are so many sounds in his environment, and yet he somehow manages to develop his own language skills without any special help.

That's one of the main reasons why most psychologists claim that your baby has an innate ability to learn language, that he arrives in the world already preprogrammed to pick out certain sound combinations from the whole array of environmental sounds that he hears. There is perhaps no other explanation that can satisfactorily

Left: Your baby's first identifiable step toward speech is a cooing sound.

account for how he spontaneously learns to speak amidst the noisy chaos of language around him.

Bear in mind, though, that other factors also play an important part in your baby's language development. For instance, the actual language your baby hears has a direct effect, which is why a baby raised by English-speaking parents learns English and not, say, French, and a baby raised by French-speaking parents learns French and not German. And there is also plenty of evidence from psychological research that the pace and richness of your baby's language development will be affected by the amount of language stimulation he receives from you and others in his family.

Following a Pattern

Another startling feature of language development is that virtually all babies build their language skills in the same way, using the same "building blocks" in the same order and usually at around the same time. This adds further support to the idea of the inborn nature of language.

Aside from the specific new skills that your baby develops each month in this early period of his life, you will also see his progress through linguistic phases, which include

• **nonverbal.** For the first six weeks or so, your baby cannot make any identifiable sounds. His only means of communication is through crying and other body language such as arm and leg movements, facial expressions, and eye contact.

• **cooing.** This is a meaningless repetitive vowel sound that your baby utters, usually when he is settled and contented. Starting at around 2 months and disappearing a couple of months later, cooing does not follow a pattern.

• **babbling (random).** By 5 months your infant can produce a wider

Below: Once your baby starts to babble, more hard consonant sounds will emerge.

range of sounds, largely because his voice and breathing have matured. Random babbling is the distinctive set of sounds your baby makes when he has your attention.

- **babbling (controlled).** For the next few months, he babbles in a more controlled way, almost as though he is taking part in a conversation with you. He may tend to use the same string of sounds regularly (such as "papapa").
- **early speech.** Toward the end of the first year, your baby makes sounds as though he is talking – he looks at you, has a serious expression on his face, and varies his voice tone – but he doesn't yet use any distinguishable words.
- **first word.** Around his twelfth month, your heart skips a beat with excitement on hearing his first word. His vocabulary will increase by ten words or so in the next few months, extending to about 50 words by around 18 months.

There is no established link between early talking and intelligence. However, early language development will give your child a head start when it comes to communicating with other people and learning from them.

Right: Reading with your child from an early age will help his vocabulary to grow.

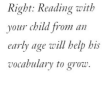

Listening and Speaking

Remember that your child uses language in two ways. First, he listens to the sounds he hears and interprets them in his own way. Known as receptive language, these analytical language skills enable him to make sense of the sounds he hears. Secondly, your infant also has expressive skills that enable him to make sounds of his own so that he can communicate verbally with you. When stimulating your baby's communication ability, focus both on his expressive language and on his receptive language.

Almost certainly your infant's receptive language will constantly remain far ahead of his expressive language. In other words, he will understand a lot more words than he can actually say. For instance, you'll discover that he smiles when he hears his name even though he can't actually say his name himself. This difference probably occurs because a growing baby typically

Above: These two babies clearly are communicating with each other, despite the fact that they cannot yet talk.

hears language long before he is mature enough to speak (when, for example, he listens to you talking to someone else), and he is encouraged to respond to language even when he hasn't the ability to speak (when, for example, you ask him if he is happy after he has been bathed and changed).

Language

Age	Skill
1 week	She pays attention to language sounds even though she can't make any of her own and tries to look at the person speaking the words.
1 month	Your baby now has a wider range of cries that she uses in different situations, depending on her mood and feeling of comfort.
2 months	For the first time your infant begins to use a couple of distinct sounds, although they don't carry any meaning and simply reflect her relaxed feelings at that time.
3 months	Her listening skills have improved, and she is much more attentive to distinctive sounds that she hears.
4 months	As part of her increased repertoire of communication skills, your baby can now give a definite laugh when something amuses her.
5 months	Her vocal cords, voice muscles, and breathing have developed to the point where she can make an increased range of sounds.
6 months	Her pre-speech is no longer randomly generated according to her mood but becomes linked to you or to other people who are familiar to her.
7 months	Her increased understanding of the meaning of language allows her to become more responsive to the content of your speech.

From Birth to 7 Months

What to Do

Hold your new baby in your arms and let her settle there. Then talk softly to her about anything that comes to mind. Watch closely as she tries to move and turn her body in response to your speech, in an attempt to tune in to the sounds she hears.

Listen very carefully when your baby cries and you will gradually build up awareness of the cry that tells you she is hungry, which is different from the cry that tells you she is bored. As you respond to her cries, tell her what you think her crying means.

Put your baby in her crib and give her a couple of toys to play with. Once she is busy with them, talk gently to her. You'll probably find that after a moment or two she starts to make sounds of her own, such as "goo," over and over again.

Lay her in her crib and let her play quietly with her toys. Move out of her line of vision. While she plays with her toys, make a small sound (such as clicking two wooden bricks together or ringing a small bell). She'll stop playing and listen to it.

Sit her on your lap with her back against you, and hold her hands on the handles of a child-safe mirror. Raise the mirror so that she sees only her own reflection, then slowly let her see your grinning face in the mirror, too. She'll howl with delight.

When you listen to her sounds you'll realize that she can make at least three or four babbling sounds. These will not appear in any order, but they will usually involve a consonant–vowel combination, which she will then repeat (such as "nananana").

Talk to your infant as you normally do. However, make a point of pausing every so often, just as you would when talking to another adult. She will start to synchronize her speech with yours, rather like taking turns in a proper conversation.

When engaged in a routine activity with your infant, such as bathing her or feeding her, make a comment that requires a response (such as "Look at that"). Her subsequent action will confirm that she has understood your remark.

Language

Age	Skill
8 months	Your baby enjoys playing language games with you, particularly those that require her to imitate the sounds that you make.
9 months	Her hearing is much more accurate, and she will scan the room to find the exact source of a sound that has attracted her attention.
10 months	Her babbling has become more sophisticated, to the point where she can actually combine different syllables in one utterance.
11 months	She can listen to you very carefully and then follow an instruction that you have given her, as long as it is within her ability.
1 year	Some children have said their first word before they reach the age of 1 year, but the majority achieve that skill around this time.
13 months	Although she can't say her name yet, she has little difficulty recognizing it when another person says it within her hearing range.
14 months	Your toddler uses her increasing vocabulary to become an active participant in games involving language, and in songs.
15 months	She can say a wider range of single words (perhaps at least five or six) and understands a lot more than that.

From 8 to 15 Months

What to Do

Put your baby in a sitting position on the floor and sit facing her. Hold her hands in yours, gently swinging them back and forth. While doing this make babbling sounds yourself (such as "babababa"). Your infant will watch you and then imitate you.

Let your child sit on the floor, or in her high chair, and give her some toys to play with. Once she is totally engrossed in her play, bring a ticking watch to her ear without her seeing you do this. She'll immediately turn around to look at the watch.

Chat to your child whenever you can and listen very carefully to the range of sounds she makes. You'll notice that she now links syllables to form a string, such as "ah-leh" or "muh-gah." There is no set pattern to these sound combinations.

Sit her in a secure comfortable chair and move toward the door as though you are about to leave the room. Turn around, wave to her, and say "Bye bye." Then ask her to wave goodbye to you. She will know what you want and start to wave her hand.

Point to a familiar person (either you or your partner), or to the family pet, and ask your 1-year-old, "Who's that?" Chances are she will say something that closely resembles the word you would have used – this is her first word.

While your child is with you, talk to another adult. Once you are sure she has begun to occupy herself by playing with some toys, say her name during the conversation. Even if you say it quietly, she will turn around to look at you.

Sing her favorite song to her, but leave out the last word of a line. She will make a valiant effort to say it. However, make sure you give her plenty of time to say the missing word before you start the next line.

Count up the number of different words – there will probably be more than you thought. Give her a broader range of basic directions, which she should be able to carry out without further help, such as "Take that cookie" or "Let go of the toy."

Stimulating Language: Birth to 3 Months

Your baby cannot talk at birth. He can't even make any individual vowel or consonant sounds. But he can communicate using crying, facial expressions, and body movements. Through this nonverbal system, your baby is able to express his basic needs to you. The language stimulation you provide during this preverbal phase of his life, however, starts the long and exciting process of his own language development.

Suitable Suggestions

The best way to encourage your baby's language skills is to talk to him at every opportunity, even though he can't understand the exact meaning of everything you say to him. By chatting to him while feeding him, changing him, playing with him, or driving in the car with him, you provide a rich array of language sounds for him to listen to and (eventually) to develop for himself.

Be animated when talking to your baby during these first three months. Make eye contact whenever possible so that he can see the broad smile that accompanies your happy words, as well as the more calm expression on your face when you to lull him to sleep. He watches your gestures and body language very closely, forming a link between the words you use, the mood you are in, and your outward appearance. This sets the foundation for his own development of speech.

Don't worry that he can't possibly grasp the content of your conversation with him, especially when you talk about subjects not directly related to his immediate world. Don't feel silly speaking to your baby who is only a few months old. The fact is that every time he sees and hears you using words, he soaks up all these examples of purposeful

Below: At only 1 month old this baby's attention is fixed on his mother's face while she talks to him.

Above: At around 2 months this baby is responding to sound and beginning to vocalize.

language, preparing him for the time when he will eventually take part in conversations and express himself using the spoken word.

Songs are important, too, because they demonstrate a further use of language. They show him that words can be accompanied by a tune to create an atmosphere that is perhaps relaxed, happy, or serene. Even if you have a dreadful singing voice, sing softly to your baby. As far as he is concerned, your voice is the most wonderful sound in the world. Its familiarity and its association with the love and care you shower on him are the factors that matter so much to your young baby. Sing him gentle lullabies sometimes to help him fall asleep; sing him nursery rhymes that will grab his attention.

Below: Singing to your baby while you rock or jiggle her will also stimulate her response to language.

❖❖❖❖❖❖ Top・Tips ❖❖❖❖❖❖

1. Interpret his cries to him. If you discover that he cried because, for instance, he needed a clean diaper, you could say to him, "You were crying because your diaper was dirty but you're happy now that I've changed it."

2. At times hold him close when talking to him. Of course you should talk to him at every opportunity, but try to ensure that there are lots of times when he is close enough to focus on your eyes, face, and mouth.

3. React strongly to your baby's vocalizations. Once he starts cooing (probably around the eighth week), smile at him and talk back to him as though he is taking part in a conversation. This encourages him to continue.

4. Use play to encourage him to speak. Your baby is likely to make sounds to express his feelings when actively engaged in play. His relaxed and happy mood makes him want to vocalize.

5. Play listening games with your baby. When he lies in his crib, for instance, attract his attention by whispering to him, or by saying his name. Good listening skills are a crucial part of communication.

Q How can I learn the different meanings of my day-old baby's cries?

A Give yourself time to get to know your baby. With experience of caring for him, you'll soon be able to match a particular cry with a particular meaning; for instance, his cry that steadily builds up when he needs to be fed will be different from his more urgent, piercing cry when he is physically uncomfortable.

Q Is it all right to let my 2-month-old baby listen to the television?

A Sounds from your television set can play a part in encouraging your infant's speech and language growth. However, the beneficial effect is limited because the language he hears isn't accompanied by other nonverbal aspects of communication. Therefore, long periods of listening to the sound of the television at this age provide little help for your baby's language development.

Toys: music box, rattle, toy that makes a noise when activated or moved, baby picture book

Stimulating Language: 4 to 6 Months

Your child passes from the cooing stage to the point where she begins to babble, and suddenly you realize that she is on the road to independent speech. Her need to make sounds becomes apparent at most times of the day as she babbles when she's with you or while playing alone. Your growing baby loves the increased range of sounds that she can make.

Suitable Suggestions

During this three-month period she becomes a more active participant in your conversations with her, and she will give you the impression that she wants to join in the discussion (even though she still makes only random babbling sounds). That's why you should pause when talking to her, just as you do when chatting with an adult. You may be surprised when she babbles away to you during these short gaps.

The same applies when asking her the sort of questions to which you know she is unable to give a coherent reply. For instance, you might ask her, "Do you feel better now that you've been fed?" or "Would you like me to take you to the park?" Of course she can't reply, but leave a short pause anyway and look at her as if you expect a response. Sometimes she will babble at that moment; even if she just stares at you in total silence, your

Right: Even when she is upset your baby will calm as you talk to her soothingly.

Above: Talk to your baby during your daily activities; animated conversation from you can be a good distraction if your child is getting fed up.

Top·Tips

1. Play her music with different tempos. She begins to react to the mood of the music she hears. Fast music might make her giggle, whereas soft music may relax her and help her stop crying.

2. Sit her facing you as you talk. Hold her firmly on your knee and say (or sing) a rhyme to her. You can move your knees slowly up and down at the same time. She enjoys this activity more because she can see you clearly all the time.

3. When taking her out in the stroller, chat to her about the things she can see. Make a comment about the color of the grass or the size of the bus that just drove past you. If she stares at something in particular, make a comment about it.

4. Talk back to her. Although her babbling is meaningless to you, speak back as though she is trying to convey some special thoughts or feelings to you. You'll be accurate some of the time.

5. Model sounds for her. To increase her range of babbling combinations, introduce a new sound by holding her so that she can see your face and then utter the sound again and again. She may start to imitate you.

words and actions help develop her understanding of the concept of turn-taking in conversations.

You should also concentrate on encouraging her listening skills. When she plays in her crib, make sounds from different parts of the room, perhaps to her left, or to her right, or directly behind her. Each time you make the noise, wait for her to turn around to look at you, and give her a huge smile and a cuddle when she achieves this.

Listening activities like these sharpen her hearing and attention skills, which are essential for later speech and language development.

Reading her stories is another useful activity. The particular story that you read her between the age of 4 and 6 months doesn't matter too much (as long as it is suitable for a young child). What matters more is that you should read the story with feeling and expression, that you should alter your voice tone appropriately during the story, and that you should engage your infant's interest in it. Every few seconds look up from the storybook and check to be sure she is looking at you. If she is distracted, gently catch her attention and then proceed with the story.

Q Is it possible that my 5-month-old baby recognizes her name when I say it?

A It is highly unlikely that she genuinely knows the sound of her name. She probably turns toward you when you say her name because she is attracted by the sound. Try saying a different name to her the next time – the chances are she will turn around and look at you this time as well.

Q Can my 6-month-old baby tell my voice apart from other people's voices?

A Almost certainly she can identify your voice from all the other voices that she hears. Your baby has spent so much time with you and has such a strong emotional attachment to you that your voice has a special meaning for her – and so her face breaks into a big smile.

Toys: plastic storybooks, cassette tapes with children's songs, voice tapes, noisy toys, play-mat with animal or shape patterns

Stimulating Language: 7 to 9 Months

As you listen closely to your baby's sounds, you'll notice that they seem to have a pattern to them. He might start to use the same sound combinations regularly, and he might even use them in the same situation. And that's a clear sign that his babbling is controlled, not random, that he is using language in a more purposeful way than ever before.

HEARING

Poor hearing can slow down language development because it means the growing infant can't hear the sounds he makes himself, nor can he hear the sounds that others make to him. A child who misses out on this early auditory stimulation finds learning to speak more challenging than does a child with normal hearing.

Signs that your baby might have a hearing difficulty include his slowness to respond to your voice, his lack of reaction to your voice when you are not directly in his line of vision, and his startled response when you suddenly appear in front of him (because he didn't hear your footsteps as you approached).

Suitable Suggestions

In addition to talking to your infant in your normal voice for most of the time, make a point of imitating his two-syllable utterances. Do this in a fun way as a game for a few minutes each day; he will thoroughly enjoy this activity.

When he sits in his high chair after has had his lunch (and therefore is in a good mood, ready to play with you), wait until he begins to babble, then pick one of the sound combinations he has just used and say it back to him ("la") using your usual tone of voice; smile as you do so and position your face within 10–12 inches of his. Your use of the same sounds makes him feel very good about himself.

Opinion is divided over the use of "baby words" instead of ordinary words. Some people argue that it is better, for example, to use the term "bow wow" than the word "dog" because that term is more akin to the speech that a child of this age uses and therefore will catch his attention quickly. But others argue that the danger with this strategy is that the child will learn the "baby word" first and then will have to relearn the proper word later on when his speech skills are more mature.

To be on the safe side, therefore, it is perhaps best just to use the proper word right from the start when talking to your infant. There is no need to use "baby words"

Below: Repetitive hiding and peek-a-boo games get an enthusiastic response.

Above: By repeatedly naming objects for your child, she will build up an understanding of words and meanings long before she can speak.

✦✦✦✦✦✦ Top·Tips ✦✦✦✦✦✦

1. Let him blow bubbles. During the day, there will be moments when he blows bubbles with his saliva while making accompanying sounds. Although you might find this habit annoying, it actually helps strengthen his lip muscles.

2. Recite "noise" rhymes. Tell your child a rhyme that has, for instance, animal sounds in it, such as "Old MacDonald's Farm." He'll have fun listening to you and may even try to copy sounds.

3. Play peek-a-boo games. This enjoyable activity involves you suddenly appearing from behind your hands, which are covering your face, and enhances your child's concentration and attention skills as he tries to anticipate your appearance.

4. Watch his favorite video with him. Sit with him as he spends a few minutes watching the video. But make sure that you talk to him instead of just sitting there quietly. Discuss the characters and events of the video as they arise.

5. Use individual picture cards. Buy or make plain cards with a picture of an object on each one. Show these to your infant, one at a time, and name each picture as he looks at it. Don't do this for more than a couple of minutes each day.

at all because he has the innate ability to pick out the key words from your speech.

Remember to name everyday household objects as you use them. It's easy to assume that there is no point in saying them because he is not yet ready to associate specific words with specific objects. Evidence from psychological research indicates that a 9-month-old child may in fact understand a lot more than he is generally given credit for. Try this out for yourself. Ask him, "Where is the spoon?" and watch his eyes. If he understands what you have said, he will start to look for the named item.

Below: Picture books are an excellent learning aid and your child will soon begin to recognize familiar images.

Q My son is almost 9 months old and I'm sure his language is developing more slowly than his sister's when she was that age. Is that normal?

A Evidence from research suggests that in general boys develop language at a slower rate than girls at every step along the way. This is a trend, however, and doesn't mean that every boy develops at a slower rate. However, it does suggest that your daughter's faster language acquisition is normal.

Q My son is 7 months old. When he babbles, he uses sounds that aren't part of our language. Why is this?

A Investigations have found that babies from countries with different languages tend to have the same range of babbling sounds (including speech sounds they haven't heard before). Your baby will eventually focus on the sounds that are relevant to your language.

🧸🚂 **Toys:** child-safe mirror, soft chewy ball, stick-on rattle for high chair, soft storybook, music tapes and CDs

Stimulating Language: 10 to 12 Months

Your child has now reached that period in her life when she will probably manage to say her first word. This is a major step forward because it signifies her ability to use spoken language in a way that allows her to communicate meaningfully and precisely with you. Your child's first spoken word also marks the start of a rapid growth in vocabulary over the next couple of years.

PACIFIERS

Sucking a pacifier can make your child feel relaxed and contented. When she has this in her mouth, though, it prevents her from using her mouth muscles, lips, and tongue to make sounds, and therefore it doesn't make any positive contribution to her speech and language development.

If your child likes sucking a pacifier, try to decrease the amount of time she spends with it in her mouth during the day. There's no harm in her using it occasionally when she is distressed or when she wants to nod off to sleep. Bear in mind, however, that extensive use of a pacifier stops her from making these all-important prespeech babbling sounds.

Suitable Suggestions

Provide good examples of speech for your child to copy. When you notice that she tends to use the same sound groupings to describe the same person or object – even though what she utters is nothing like the proper word – encourage her by saying the word she means. For instance, if she excitedly makes the sound "paneh" whenever she sees her grandmother, you could say to her, "Yes, that's right, it's Grandma." Although her utterance and your word might appear to be totally different from your point of view, your child might think they are the same. So your speech provides a model for her to copy.

But don't pressure her into saying her first word, or you may end up discouraging her language development. At this age, your child's sounds should be spontaneous, not forced, and should be made because she wants to communicate with you, not because she thinks you will be disappointed with her if she doesn't speak. Of course, every parent of a child this age looks for the sound grouping that could be classed as a word. Yet there is a difference between waiting for a word in excited anticipation and making your child anxious because she hasn't yet managed to meet your expectations.

Songs and nursery rhymes should play an increased role in her daily routine. By now

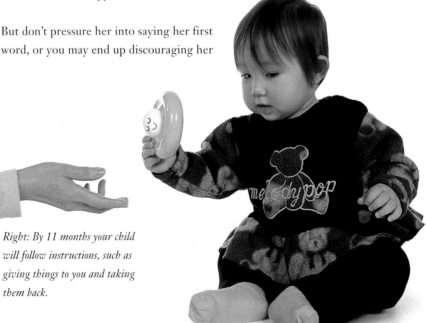

Right: By 11 months your child will follow instructions, such as giving things to you and taking them back.

she is totally familiar with the words and tunes, and she tries to "sing" along with you in her own way. This activity not only enhances her listening skills but also teaches her the sequential nature of language. In other words she learns that speech follows a sequence and isn't just a random series of sounds. Show her how pleased you are when she tries to join in.

Listen to her attentively, too. She needs to know that you focus on her speech sounds, just as you expect her to listen to you.

Above: Another milestone in your child's understanding is when she starts to enjoy the progression of a story rather than just picture books.

Make good eye contact with your toddler when she speaks, match your facial expression to hers, listen without unnecessary interruptions, and then respond as though you fully understood the message she tried to convey. This is the precursor to genuine verbal conversation.

Below: Musical toys help your child's aural development and encourage her to experiment with different sounds.

✦✦✦✦✦✦✦ Top·Tips ✦✦✦✦✦✦✦

1. Talk to her throughout the day. Your infant still benefits from hearing you use language purposefully in everyday settings, either addressed to her or when you talk to other people. This basic stimulation helps extend her vocabulary.

2. Give her toy musical instruments. She'll love crashing the toy drum with the sticks, and she will devise her own vocal accompaniment to go along with that activity. Making up songs of her own is good fun, and she never tires of this.

3. Expect her to respond to basic instructions. Ask your year-old toddler to "Give me the spoon." Reward a positive response with a smile or hug; if she doesn't understand, repeat the question, then lift up the spoon to show her.

4. Cuddle up together when watching a video or television. As she snuggles up to you, talk in a gentle voice about the program or video, perhaps describing the main characters. Her relaxed mood makes her listen closely.

5. Read her a bedtime story. Your toddler will settle better at night when you sit on her bed to read her a story. She concentrates on every word you say in that situation because she is happy and there are no other distractions.

Q Why is it that a young child's first word is nearly always "mom" or "dad?"

A That often happens simply because parents spend a great deal of time with their child, making them the most familiar adults in her world. However, a child's first word might easily be the name of the family pet or the term she uses to describe her favorite cuddly toy.

Q How aware is a 1-year-old of other people's names?

A In addition to recognizing her own name when she hears it, she probably knows the names of other people in her family and the names of other familiar adults, such as her day care provider or nanny. When she is with you and her brothers and sisters, speak one of their names. You'll find that she turns to look at that child before he speaks.

🧸🚂 **Toys:** wind-up music toy, storybooks with basic pictures, plastic toy animal, toy telephone, cuddly soft toy

Stimulating Language: 13 to 15 Months

If your child didn't start to speak before the end of his first year, he will almost certainly have achieved this milestone by the time he reaches his fifteenth month. He can say several words himself and understands the meaning of hundreds more, though there is one word that probably always results in a negative reaction from him – and that's when you say "no!"

Every child develops at her own rate, and although the majority of children have said their first word by the time they reach 15 months, a significant number don't achieve this stage until a few months later.

So there is no need to be unduly concerned about the nonappearance of the first word, especially if there are other signs that her speech is developing in a normal way. For instance, the presence of babbling is a positive sign that her language development is progressing satisfactorily, as is her active involvement in songs and nursery rhymes.

Left: At this age a child will enjoy familiar rhymes and action songs.

the sole of his foot when you explain that "This is your foot." Do this each night, though try not to make it so routine that he becomes bored with it. Simple games like this help him learn the names of these body parts.

Suitable Suggestions
Now is a good time to introduce pretend play to your toddler, using his cuddly toys. Set them up in a circle and pretend to talk to them. At first, your toddler aged between 13 and 15 months might stare at you in amazement or burst out laughing. But he'll soon realize this is good fun and will join in as best he can. Do this with him a couple of times and you'll discover that he plays this game with his cuddly toys on his own; you'll hear him chatting away to himself and his toys.

When you bathe or change your toddler, start to name his body parts. Make this a fun activity, perhaps by tickling his hand when you tell him, "This is your hand" or tickling

Right: Use everyday routines to name commonplace objects such as shoes. Your child will soon learn these words.

If possible, arrange for your toddler to spend some time in the company of other children who are approximately the same age (though it won't matter if they are a few months older). He won't play with them, but he will be fascinated by their use of language. Most children this age want to be like other children and do every single thing they can to imitate them, so the company of other children can indirectly stimulate his language development.

Left: At 15 months your toddler may well hold conversations with his soft toys.

❖❖❖❖❖ Top·Tips ❖❖❖❖❖

1. Start to name individual colors. Your child is a long way from being able to identify and name the main colors. However, you won't do any harm by starting the process off now, and you may help him differentiate between colors.

2. Show excitement at every new word your toddler says. Pay close attention to the words he uses so that you know when a new word has crept into his vocabulary. He is delighted with your approval of his latest achievement.

3. Get your toddler actively involved with objects you name. Do this where possible because it is very effective. For instance, he'll learn the name of a ball more quickly when he plays with it rather than just staring passively at it.

4. Use lots of repetition. Be prepared to say the same things over and over again. Of course you don't want your discussion with your toddler to be boring for him, but repetition of object names facilitates the language learning process.

5. Play with finger puppets. Your 15-month-old child loves finger puppets, especially when you move them about and make them talk to him. He will try to talk back to them. This is a fun, imaginative activity that stretches his language.

Your child will still use gestures as part of his communication, even though his verbal skills steadily increase. You can help his speech progress by resisting the temptation to respond to his gestures alone. For instance, should he point at his cup of juice, ask him "Do you want the cup of juice?" or even better, "What is it you want?" Repeat the question if he continues to point. Eventually he will try to communicate his desire using spoken sounds instead of gestures alone.

Left: Start to name colors for your child, though it will be quite a long time before he grasps this concept.

Q & A

Q My 5-year-old is very fond of his 15-month-old sister and tends to speak for her. Should I discourage this?

A Yes. Gently explain to your older child that you are so pleased he wants to help his sister, but that she needs to learn to speak herself. Suggest that the best way he can help her is to let her try to speak, even if it isn't easy for her. Your 5-year-old will understand this.

Q Why do most children come out with single words to start with whereas others start with phrases from the outset?

A This is another example of the wide variations that can occur as part of normal development. Just as most children crawl before they walk whereas a few go straight to walking without crawling, the same stage-jumping can happen with language, too.

🧸🚂 **Toys:** pop-up toy, toy musical instruments and musical toys, plastic train, tape of animal noises, soft toys and dolls

Learning

The Development of Learning Skills

Your baby learns so much in her first 15 months that you couldn't write it down even if you tried! From a baby who knows absolutely nothing about the world into which she is launched, she becomes an active learner who interprets, thinks, makes decisions, and remembers. The transformation is totally amazing.

Above: A baby's natural curiosity means he will constantly seek out new learning experiences for himself.

The main way in which she develops her innate learning ability is through play. It doesn't matter whether she plays with a rattle, with her crib blanket, with her food, with her hands, with the bathwater, or in fact anything at all – the fact is that when she interacts playfully

Below: Many quite ordinary objects provide an opportunity for a child to explore.

with anything in her environment she learns new things. Look on her as a dynamic scientist who just can't wait to get out there to explore everything.

For your young baby, every new experience represents a new and exciting discovery. To you, for instance, emptying the laundry from the machine into the laundry basket is so routine that you probably don't even think about it, but to your baby it is totally engrossing. She soaks up everything she sees and in doing so improves her learning skills every single day of her life.

A good way to define learning ability (also called "intelligence," "learning skills," "thinking skills," and "cognition') is your baby's ability to learn new skills and concepts, make sense of events that happen around her, use her memory

accurately, and solve small problems.

I'm Ready

When your baby is born, she already has a wide range of learning skills that ensure she is ready to explore and discover, such as

• **visual discrimination.** Within hours of birth, a new baby can tell the difference between your face and the face of a stranger. She can also tell the difference between a picture of a real face and a picture of a face in which the components are mixed up.

• **touch discrimination.** Soon after birth, she responds differently to hairbrush hairs of different diameters – in other words, she knows a thick hair feels different from a thin hair. In addition, she will respond to a puff of air that is so gentle that even you couldn't feel it.

• **taste discrimination.** Your new baby also has a good sense of taste and smell. She makes a distinctive facial expression when she tastes foods that are sweet, sour, or bitter. These facial expressions are the same ones that adults make when they experience these tastes.

• **reach discrimination.** Your new-born baby's movements of her hands and arms are not simply random movements. In one study, young babies wore special glasses

Above: Toys that do lots of different things will fascinate an older baby – though they can lose their novelty quite quickly.

that made them see an object that did not exist. Not only did the babies reach for the item, but they cried when they discovered it wasn't actually there.

• **hearing discrimination.** She can tell one cry from another. For instance, research has found that typically a new baby cries when she hears another baby cry, whereas she tends to stop crying when she hears a recording of her own crying. She also prefers the sound of a human voice to any other sound.

It's evidence like this that confirms your baby is ready to learn, right from birth. These (and other) basic learning skills provide the foundation for all her future learning, and from that moment and throughout her first 15 months, your baby's thirst for new knowledge, understanding, and information never stops.

The Source of Learning Skills

Nobody knows for sure where your child's learning ability comes from, though there are two main competing explanations:

• **inherited.** Since your baby has many characteristics inherited from you (for example, her eye coloring, her height), it stands to reason that some of her learning ability is also

inherited from you. Studies have found, for instance, that identical twins have levels of intelligence that are more closely matched than those of nonidentical twins. However, it is impossible to quantify the exact contribution that heredity makes to your child's learning ability.

• **acquired.** There is endless evidence – both from scientific studies and from commonsense everyday life – that a baby learns through experience and that the quality of her learning ability depends on the quality of her learning experiences in the early years. This theory suggests that the level of stimulation provided for your baby in this initial stage of her life will greatly influence her learning skills; offering her a wide range of play opportunities enhances her learning ability.

The true explanation probably lies somewhere in between these two extremes. Your child's intelligence or learning ability is more likely to result from the interaction between the learning skills that she brings into the world at birth and the interesting experiences she encounters as she grows. That's why it is important to view your growing

Right: At around 15 months a child will quickly be able to work out how a simple toy operates, even if he has never seen it before.

baby as an active learner, as someone who is ready to learn but needs you to stimulate and challenge her existing abilities. The interaction between you and your baby boosts her learning skills.

Remember that your baby learns best in a relaxed atmosphere. A baby whose efforts at learning and discovering are greeted by an indifferent or overanxious parent will soon lose her motivation to learn further. Playing and learning has to be fun for everyone involved.

Learning

Age	Skill
1 week	From the wide array of sounds and sights that make up his immediate environment, he is able at times to focus his attention. 
1 month	Your baby loves to look at anything that comes within his line of vision, especially when it is close to his face.
2 months	He can control his vision more accurately and will peer with interest at an object that moves in a pattern in front of him.
3 months	Your baby's learning ability has increased to the point where he can see a link between his behavior and a particular reaction.
4 months	His memory increases to the extent where he can recall how to play with a particular toy in a particular way.
5 months	His increased confidence in his ability to explore and learn makes him an active learner whenever he has the opportunity.
6 months	He begins to recognize himself when he sees his image in a photograph or in a mirror. He likes you to say who the image represents.
7 months	His memory has advanced so that he is able to remember faces of adults whom he does not see very frequently.

From Birth to 7 Months

What to Do

Hold your new baby in your hands so that he faces you with his head roughly 7–9 inches away from yours. His eyes will look at you initially, then wander. When you gently say his name, his eyes will turn back to you.

Watch him as he lies quietly in his crib. You'll notice that eventually he plays with his fingers. Maybe he wiggles them about, maybe he puts them into his mouth, or maybe he just fans the air with them. His hands and fingers fascinate him.

Take a small crib toy and tie it at one end of a piece of string that is about 12 inches long. Dangle this toy in front of your baby until his attention is attracted, then move it in a sweeping circular motion. His eyes will stay with the toy as it travels in the circle.

When your baby is lying comfortably in his crib, talk to him so that he watches you. Then gently place a clean tissue over his face, but keep talking so he knows you are still there. You'll see him move his body around until the tissue falls off.

Take an activity toy – with several different moving parts – and show your infant how to operate one of the parts. Let him play with this for a couple of minutes, then remove the toy for two or three days. When you give him the toy again, he will recall what to do.

Securely fasten your infant into his high chair and fit the tray on tightly. Now put a wide array of small toys on the tray. You will see him reach for all of them in turn, playing with each of them until he loses interest and turns to the next one.

Give him a nonglass child-safe mirror that has chunky handles on either side. Put his hands around it and then gently bring the mirror into his line of vision until he stares straight into it. You will see him stare closely and then give a big smile.

Watch your baby's face very closely at the arrival of a familiar adult who hasn't been near him for at least a couple of days (for instance, the baby-sitter or a relative). You'll see him become excited at the moment of recognition.

Learning

Age	Skill
8 months	He understands that an object still exists even though it is concealed, and he tries to look for it.
9 months	Materials engage his interest. He loves to feel the textures and explore the possibilities of making new shapes and sounds with them.
10 months	Your child grasps the concept of imitation, that he can observe an action by you and then make an attempt to copy it.
11 months	His concentration has matured so that he can focus on an activity for at least a minute or so without letting his attention wander.
1 year	He understands basic directions, as long as they are straightforward and involve only one action that is within his capability.
13 months	No longer content to be passive during feeding, he wants to get involved and perhaps even take charge of his own meals.
14 months	He can complete a simple but lengthy task, as long as you give him regular encouragement along the way.
15 months	Your child is able to combine his hand–eye control, his concentration, his memory, and his understanding to complete a complex task.

From 8 to 15 Months

What to Do

Let your 8-month-old infant see you put a small toy under a cup, right in front of him. Ask him, "Where's the toy?" As soon as you have finished the question, he will put his hand out to lift up the cup. He will smile at the success of his search.

Put a piece of paper on his tray when he is sitting in the high chair, or beside him on the floor as he sits. Your infant will pick up the paper, then crumple it before throwing it back on the floor. Don't leave important documents lying around!

Sit your infant on the floor so that you face each other. Smile and gently clap your hands together, again and again, though not so loudly, that he blinks. He will try to clap his own hands together, despite his lack of coordination.

Sit your child on your knee and let him watch the pages of his favorite picture book as you turn them over. He will stare intently at the pictures, without losing interest, and might even point to them occasionally.

Make an elementary request such as, "Give me the toy." He will grasp the meaning of your intention, actively scan his surroundings for the toy, and then hand it to you. You could also ask him to "Wave bye-bye."

Although the process will always be messy at this age, do allow your 13-month-old child to use a spoon in his attempt to feed himself. Of course some will fall off, but he is determined to gain more control in this situation.

Give him a large cup and a pile of small wooden beads (though watch that he doesn't put them in his mouth). Put one bead into the cup, then another, and then ask him to do the same. He'll put in at least half a dozen before getting fed up.

Seat your child in a comfortable child-sized chair at a table. Build a small tower with wooden bricks, right in front of him. Then give him some bricks and ask him to do the same. Depending on his mood, he might build a tower around three blocks high.

Stimulating Learning: Birth to 3 Months

It's true that your baby spends much of her day either eating or sleeping – or crying! But don't let that fool you. In these first three months, she is desperate to learn new skills and new information. She stares at everything she sees, trying to understand it; better still, she prefers hands-on experience because that's a more effective way for her to learn.

COLOR AND SHAPE RECOGNITION

It's strange to think that your baby is such a sophisticated learner that she can tell the difference between colors, but she can! Experiments have found that when a new baby is shown various colors one at a time, she stares longer at blue and green objects than she does at red ones. Color preference is present early on.

The same applies with shapes. The length of time she stares at different shapes confirms that she can discriminate between a circle, a triangle, a cross, and a square. Psychologists don't know for sure what she actually sees, but she definitely is able to differentiate between those four shapes.

Above: Even small babies may be soothed by familiar music.

Suitable Suggestions

Take nothing for granted. Instead, assume that everything your baby sees and does actually develops her learning skills that much further. Playing with her and talking to her as you clean and change her, for instance, engages her curiosity. She watches the diaper appear and tries to work out how it arrived there, she feels the sensation of the cleaning lotion and talcum powder on her bottom, and she gasps in wonderment at the way her clothes are put on her. There's so much to learn from life's daily routines.

Her vision is already set to focus at around 7 inches. Hold her about that distance from your face while resting her in one arm, then gently move a toy back and forth in the space between your face and hers. In addition to encouraging her to focus on the

toy, this brings the object so close to her face that her natural inquisitiveness is stimulated. You'll find that she wriggles in your arms to indicate her interest, even though she isn't mature enough to reach out for the toy.

Make sure she has a wide range of brightly colored noisy toys whenever she rests in her crib or carriage. Obviously you shouldn't make her space too crowded (or she may not be able to focus on any one toy in particular) but she likes to have two or three different

Below: Although you won't be aware of it, babies can distinguish different colors and shapes from birth.

Left: One of the first signs that your baby is learning is when she smiles in response to your face and voice.

toys close by her. And there's no harm in one of them being a cuddly toy – she learns just as much from that as from any other play object. Cuddly toys teach her about texture, size, and movement.

Crib mobiles play a large part in the life of your baby at this age. Since much of your new baby's explorations are visual rather than tactile (because she isn't yet able to reach out for toys that attract her attention), she likes to look at

an interesting array of toys hanging above her crib. She learns a great deal by peering at them as they turn in different directions, showing her different perspectives each time. Choose a brightly colored mobile, preferably one with lots of different attachments rather than one with several variations on the same theme. As it gently rotates on the supporting string, each new image delights your baby.

Below: Noisy, bright, and textured toys are ideal for a small baby.

◆◆◆◆◆◆◆ Top·Tips ◆◆◆◆◆◆◆

1. Spend time playing and talking with her whenever you can. Your baby learns from you playing with her just as much as she does from playing on her own. At this stage, she depends on you to initiate some play activities.

2. Don't worry about overstimulating your baby. Obviously you want to avoid making her so excited that she bursts out crying, but that is unlikely. She wants as much stimulation and fun as you can have with her.

3. Remember that she is an active learner even at this age. No matter what you do with her, she will interpret your actions and reactions in her own way. She doesn't simply lie there passively, watching aimlessly as the world drifts by.

4. Let her play with the same toys the next day, too. Variety is important, but your baby learns new things each time she plays with the same toy as she holds it and looks at it in a different way.

5. Have confidence in yourself. Since your baby at this stage learns a great deal from everyday interactions with you, be confident that you are providing a satisfactory level of stimulation for her.

LEARNING

Q Should my young baby be able to imitate some of my actions?

A To some extent, yes. If you stand at the foot of your baby's crib and complete an action that you know she is already capable of (such as opening and closing her mouth, or thrusting her tongue forward), chances are she will carry out this action more frequently just after she has seen you do it.

Q Should I talk and smile while I am playing with my young baby or will that distract her attention?

A Her attention will be momentarily drawn to you, but that mild negative effect is greatly outweighed by the pleasure she receives from your attention. And if she is happy and contented because you show an interest in her, she is in a better frame of mind to discover and learn.

Stimulating Learning: 4 to 6 Months

One of the most noticeable changes in your infant's learning ability between the ages of 3 and 6 months is that he is more adventurous, with a sharper interest in objects that are not immediately beside him. It's as though his perspective on life broadens as he realizes there really is a big wide world out there. And his increased hand and arm control allows him to reach out and grasp, opening a whole new set of learning experiences.

LEARNING BEHAVIOR

Your growing baby also learns to make associations when it comes to human behavior. Resist the temptation to underestimate his abilities. For instance, by now he has learned that shouting or crying can be an effective way to get your attention; most parents respond instantly to a crying baby. And they are quite right to do so.

Yet some times it's worth waiting a couple of seconds or so before responding. That way your baby will also learn how to deal with situations on his own. Of course, if he is crying from hunger, he needs to eat. However, if he cries from boredom then a slight delay before you go to him helps your infant learn how to seek his own amusement actively.

Suitable Suggestions

Since the ability to concentrate is fundamental to learning (because even the brightest child won't learn unless he can focus long enough to absorb new information), you can begin to extend your infant's attention span. In the first few months, he used his attention passively, in that he would look at an object only when it was exactly in front of him. By the time he has reached 5 or 6 months, however, your growing infant has greater control and can actively search for objects.

Right: Once your baby is happy playing on his front, a toy placed just out of reach will encourage him to stretch for it.

Practice this with him. Let him watch you, say, put his teddy bear on a chair that is in another part of the room but that he can see. Play with him for a few minutes, then ask,

Below: An activity center attached to the side of your baby's crib can provide valuable stimulation, even when you are not there.

Above: Once your child can sit up, it is much easier for her to manipulate toys in a variety of ways.

"Where's the teddy bear?" He will actively scan for the object. If he can't find it, try again. And if he still can't find the teddy bear, repeat all the actions, making sure that he can see you place the bear on the chair.

Don't waste your time searching for so-called "educational toys." At this stage, every toy is educational in that your infant learns from anything he plays with. That's why the cardboard box that the expensive toy came in is of more interest to your child than the toy itself! Its bright colors, smooth surface, and moving cardboard lid teach him about shape, texture, color, and movement. You could end up spending a lot of money on toys that don't actually enhance your child's learning skills.

Encourage him to explore once he gets his hands on a toy. Maybe he is one of those rather timid children who prefers a quiet environment. If so, demonstrate that the toy can be shaken, bashed against the side of the crib, or even thrown on the floor. Maybe he holds the object in only one position all the time. If so, regularly turn the toy gently in his hands so that he begins to see the value of taking a more active approach to his learning. Maybe he makes a fuss when you give him a new toy because he prefers the ones he already has. If so, take the new toy to him, play with him until he is comfortable with it, and then make sure he plays with that toy occasionally along with the other familiar ones. Stretch his learning horizons.

Below: If your child seems bored with his toys, improvise. Paper or a cardboard box will prove just as interesting to him.

✦✦✦✦✦✦✦ Top·Tips ✦✦✦✦✦✦✦

1. Let him play in a sitting position. Although he still needs support for sitting, he will play differently with toys in that position than when he lies down. His varied body posture allows him to use his hands and arms in different ways.

2. Give him age-appropriate toys. The manufacturers' age guidelines do not apply to every single child but they are generally accurate. There's no point in giving him a toy for a much older child — he won't know what to do with it.

3. Provide cause-and-effect toys. Your infant is now at an age when he begins to see the connection between his behavior and a reaction from the toy (as long as that reaction is a reasonably loud noise or a bright light).

4. Reinforce his play with your smiles and attention. You'll notice that he looks up at you while playing, especially when he completes something new. In that situation, let him know how pleased you are with his achievement.

5. Make obvious start-of-routine actions. To encourage his ability to predict events, make the first step of a familiar routine very obvious (for instance, loudly get his bath towel from the cupboard) and watch his anticipatory reaction.

Q & A

Q My 6-month-old loves to throw toys out of his carriage. Is it a good idea to tie them on to a piece of ribbon?

A You need to be very careful when using this strategy because there is a potential danger that your baby could wrap the ribbon around his neck. So you would have to keep it shorter than 6 inches. A better idea is to give his toy back a couple of times, then put it away in your pocket.

Q When my baby plays, should I turn off the radio to avoid distractions?

A Certainly you could turn down the volume, but there is no need to turn off the radio altogether. He needs to develop the ability to screen out distractions while learning, so this is good practice for him at the moment. Anyway, the background music may relax him and consequently could make his learning more enjoyable.

Toys: wooden cubes, baby gym, crib activity center, nesting cups, noisy blocks, wobbly toy, bath toy, box that rattles

Stimulating Learning:
7 to 9 Months

Your infant's newfound crawling skills mean that she can extend her sphere of learning and discovery to new territories. That's why you'll suddenly find that she has thrust her hand deep into the video player. It's not that she is being deliberately naughty, just that she is eager to find out what goes on inside that mysterious gap that takes the tape. Now she can move over to it to learn for herself.

Look, I'm Doing It

One of the hallmarks of this period in your child's life is that she gradually realizes she can have a direct effect on her surroundings and that something she does will influence an object that is not actually in her hands. She learns in an elementary way the nature of cause and effect and puts this into practice.

Don't be surprised, therefore, to see your 9-month-old infant pulling at a rug to obtain the toy that rests on the far side of it. In her mind, she has established the complex connection between pulling the rug and bringing the desired object closer. This new learning concept gives her more control over her environment.

Suitable Suggestions

Your 8-month-old baby often finds objects more interesting when they are farther away from her. The unknown aspect of that far-away toy grabs her curiosity, making her want to learn more about it. That's why you find her straining herself to reach a knickknack on a raised shelf. She can't resist the lure of the unknown. So play "come and get it" games to encourage her thirst for learning. You could shake a box with a toy inside, making it rattle, then place the box a few feet away from her. Her desperation to find out what's inside motivates her to crawl and open the box.

Of course your infant likes to sit on the floor surrounded by her toys, but her innate need to learn means that she is always ready to look farther afield for new discoveries.

Below: It is intriguing to watch a baby responding to an image that she does not yet recognize as being her own reflection.

Right: A baby is learning about sound, texture, and coordination when she does something as simple as banging two plastic rings together.

When you do try to keep her from exploring, she will probably be furious with you. Clearly you have to set limits, but you also have to be careful not to discourage her from developing her learning skills. This isn't always easy. Sometimes a compromise can be reached. For instance, you could let her hold the clock so that she can look at it closely, while making sure that you retain a firm grip on it, too. Then put it back in its usual place. That way her curiosity may be satisfied without giving her free rein to explore wherever she wants.

Remember, too, that your infant still learns from playing with familiar toys. Perhaps she has had a large soft ball for a couple of months and whenever she gets hold of it she simply chews it or drops it out of her hands. At the age of 8 or 9 months, however, she might learn something new: for instance, that she can hit it against the wall and it comes back to her, that it bounces if dropped from a height, that unless the surface is perfectly flat the ball doesn't sit still when placed there. In other words, she learns new things from old toys. So encourage her to play with all her toys, not just the ones you bought her most recently.

Below: Let your baby experiment with her food from time to time.

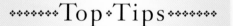

✦✦✦✦✦✦✦ Top·Tips ✦✦✦✦✦✦✦

1. Don't restrict her too much. Of course there are safety issues to consider, but allow your baby to explore freely under supervision. If she aims for forbidden territory, gently redirect her to safer ground.

2. Play with mirrors. Even though she doesn't actually know that the image she sees in the mirror is her own, your infant still has great fun looking in a child-proof mirror. She'll squeal with delight when she sees your face appear there, too.

3. Let her sometimes make a mess when eat. Food fascinates your child because it can be molded and smeared into all sorts of shapes. At times, allow her to play with her food if she wants instead of eating it right away.

4. Continue to challenge her memory. For instance, putting her teddy bear behind your back and asking her to find it enhances her recall. And if you bring out your hand without the teddy bear in it, she will probably try to crawl behind you to get it.

5. Put her in the baby seat in the supermarket cart. Shopping without a grumpy infant is easier, yet she learns lots from cruising the aisles with you. Steer a middle course with the cart, though, to avoid her grabbing things off the shelves.

Q When my baby plays with cups in the bath, does she really learn anything?

A Yes, she does. If you observe her playing with these items, you'll see that she stares intently as she fills the cup, then empties it, then fills it again. This is the first stage in learning about volume and about the way liquids change shape depending on the containers that hold them. It's another example of free play enhancing your infant's thinking skills.

Q My child is 8 months old and doesn't seem to see very small items. Is that normal?

A Her vision is maturing all the time, but it is still not as refined or sophisticated as yours. Evidence from research suggests that at this age she can probably see an object the size of a shirt button, but anything much smaller than that is not visible to her. In the next few months, her visual skills develop further.

🧸🚂 **Toys:** toy with smaller pieces fitting into the main part, water toys, rings that stack on a pillar, balls of different sizes, empty containers

Stimulating Learning: 10 to 12 Months

What a difference a few months make to your child's learning skills! He has been able to move around and search actively for a couple of months already, but at this point he is ready to take a more focused approach to learning. Although exploration is still crucial to his learning, he spends more time playing with each individual toy than he did before, studying it more closely.

BRIGHT FIRSTBORN

A plethora of evidence confirms that the firstborn child in a family tends to be the brightest of all the children, and the effect lasts throughout childhood and into adulthood. This doesn't apply to every single firstborn child, of course, but is nevertheless an identifiable tendency.

The most likely explanation for this finding is that the firstborn child is the only one in the family to have parental attention all to himself (at least for a couple of years before the next one arrives). He has undivided parental interest, time, and resources, and this probably results in a high level of stimulation that is hard to replicate when there are two or more children to be cared for.

Suitable Suggestions

Your child's concentration and attention become more systematic. Previously he would have been all over the place, flitting from one toy to the next, scanning it briefly, playing with it briefly, then discarding it. His maturity allows him to look at objects systematically rather than randomly. You can encourage this through instructions.

Above: At this age your child is likely to recognize animals and objects in her picture books.

Sit him on your knee as you read through a picture book. Instead of flicking over the pages, one after the other in quick succession, point out the different objects and draw his attention to them. Directions such as "Look at the doll" or "Look at the cow" help train your infant to scan the entire page instead of looking just at the first thing he sees. And if he points out an object on the page, then another object, give him a big cuddle and lots of praise. Even if he doesn't pick out the images in a systematic way, wait several seconds before you turn the page.

Give him opportunities to practice existing learning skills in new situations – he is at the

Left: This 11-month-old is deliberately stacking blocks in order to knock them over.

Above: Pretend play is likely to start with an action that your child sees you do frequently.

stage where he can adapt old strategies to novel problems. For instance, suppose he likes to play with toy nesting boxes and is able to fit them into each other properly. Try to find other items that fit this way, too, such as plastic cups of various sizes or small plastic barrels. At first, he may hesitate when faced with the new puzzle, but he will soon apply his existing knowledge. Experiences like this build his confidence as a learner, making him a motivated problem-solver who can adapt and apply his learning concepts.

Encourage him to persist with those puzzle toys that he couldn't complete before, but remove the easy pieces. Shape-sorters, for instance, often contain some parts that can be fitted by a younger child (because they have the same outline no matter how they are rotated) as well as some that are usually not mastered until the child is older, by which time he may be bored with the toy altogether. So give him the shape-sorter without the easier shapes (such as the square, circle, and triangle), and suggest that he put the remaining shapes into the right places. Calm him if he becomes frustrated; cheer him on until he succeeds.

Top·Tips

1. **Keep some "special" toys.** At those times when your toddler is very bored, fed up, and whining, bring out a toy that you have kept concealed in a cupboard. The sudden introduction of this toy cheers him up and stimulates his learning.

2. **Name basic body parts.** Playfully shake his hand and say, "This is your hand." Do this for his feet, ears, nose, mouth, and tummy. He starts to associate the word with the appropriate body part.

3. **Play along with him.** Research studies have found that the presence of a parent during play usually has a number of positive effects: the child plays for longer, is more willing to try unfamiliar toys, and is more adventurous in his explorations.

4. **Start a routine, then let him continue.** This strengthens his memory. Complete the first stage of a familiar routine (for example, take out the bath towel) but stop there. Give your toddler time to continue, perhaps by starting to pull his socks off.

5. **Provide access to household utensils.** A small plastic bottle and a basin of water let him learn from water play, and a piece of dough allows him to make different shapes. He learns from playing with ordinary (but safe) household items.

Left: Persuade your child to try some of the harder shapes in the shape-sorter that she may have bypassed until now.

Q&A

Q Exactly what is an intelligence test?

A This is a series of items that claims to measure important learning skills, such as reasoning, short-term memory, long-term memory, and pattern recognition. A child's performance on these various tests is then compared against the average scores that have been previously obtained from a very large sample of children his own age.

Q Should I arrange for my child to have an intelligence test to see how bright he is?

A The problem with intelligence tests is that they don't give an accurate picture of how a child will perform in a real-life problem-solving situation – they are too artificial and may be inaccurate. That's why it is far better for you to continue stimulating your child's learning skills each day than to arrange for an intelligence test.

Stimulating Learning: 13 to 15 Months

Your child's increased hand–eye coordination skills, along with her ability to toddle all over the place, give her the confidence to investigate the entire house. You come into the kitchen one day, only to find her sitting quietly on the floor as she empties all the containers in your food cupboard. Unperturbed by the mess, her desire to learn blots out all worries about the consequences of her learning adventure.

USE HER NAME

Help develop your child's listening skills by using her name when talking to her. For instance, if you want her to play with a puzzle toy, instead of saying, "Here's a toy for you," start the sentence with her name and then wait until she has turned toward you before completing it.

The same applies to simple requests. You might have to repeat everything to your toddler, almost as though she can't be bothered with listening, yet it's more likely you have to do this because she doesn't tune in to your instruction until you are halfway through it. Saying her name at the start gains her attention, and gives her time to concentrate on what you have to say.

Suitable Suggestions

Imagination starts to play a role in your child's life for the first time, and this begins a major shift in her thinking skills. Between birth and 12 months, she could think only in terms of what she saw directly in front of her. If the toy wasn't in her line of vision she couldn't pretend it was there, and that clearly limited her learning potential. Around 12 to 15 months, she becomes capable of symbolic thought and as a result can use one object to represent another; for instance, a wooden block can be a cup that she tries to drink out of. Imagination is an important part of learning.

Start playing "pretend" games with your toddler. Reading her stories with an animated expression is one way to enhance her imagination. You can also pretend to have a tea party for her cuddly toys. She has terrific fun pretending to pour cups of tea for her guests, enabling her to practice actions that she has seen you carry out. Provide opportunities for her to use learned information in practical ways. Take tidying up, for example. This is good from several points of view, such as encouraging

Left: Include your child in the household routine. You can make tidying up fun by encouraging her to put some of her own toys away.

Left: Most toddlers will consider it a great privilege to be allowed to use some of your equipment and copy what you do.

independence and responsibility, but it also has value in developing her organizational skills. Picking up her toys requires her to search the room systematically, to remember to place toys in the same box each time she picks one up from the floor, and to concentrate on the task until it is completed. She loves helping you with this, so resist the temptation to do it all yourself even though that would complete the job at a faster rate.

You can also stimulate her creativity by setting up a small tray with a thick mixture of sand and water, though watch her closely in case she thinks it would be a good idea to taste it. Make the texture solid enough to stick together, roll up your toddler's sleeves and let her immerse her hands in the substance. At first she probably just picks up the mud, then lets it drop. Once the initial excitement is over, however, she may start to use her memory and background knowledge to create shapes, models, and patterns.

Below: Sand and water play will fascinate your child but will need supervision.

✦✦✦✦✦✦✦ Top·Tips ✦✦✦✦✦✦✦

1. Extend her play. Help her learn how to extend the way she plays. For instance, if she makes one shape with the play dough, ask her to make another shape. If she rolls the toy car in one direction, ask her to push it in another direction.

2. Point out the different body parts on a large doll. Previously you showed these on your child, but now she is able to learn them on a doll. Stick to the obvious parts, such as hair, head, eyes, feet, hands, mouth, and ears.

3. Don't pressure her. In your concern to improve her learning, you could have unrealistically high expectations of her achievements. By all means encourage her learning, but make sure the challenges you give are reasonable for her age.

4. Practice, then break, then practice. When teaching your toddler a new skill, such as completing an inset board, let her do this for a couple of minutes, play with something else, then return to the inset board again after the break.

5. Let her struggle at times. Naturally you don't want your child to explode with frustration when the toy won't work the way she wants. But if you rush in with the solution every time, she won't learn the solution herself. Find a balance.

Q What size of jigsaw puzzle should my 15-month-old toddler be able to manage?

A Most toddlers can't manage a traditional jigsaw puzzle because it is a complex challenge, even if there are only two pieces. However, she will probably be able to place a flat wooden shape back into the correct space on an inset board, assuming there is only one space (or two spaces at the most).

Q How can I stop my toddler from being so impulsive? She is so quick when playing.

A Children vary in the way they approach a learning experience. Some – like your toddler – rush through it as quickly as they can, whereas others take their time. The next time your toddler plays with a toy, sit with her and chat to her; point to the toy, engage her interest in it, and talk to her about it. This slows her down in her play, helping her be more reflective.

🧸 🚂 **Toys:** play dough, sand and water tray, plastic shapes, inset board, action toy, plastic tea set, Duplo/Lego

Social and

Emotional
Development

Social and Emotional Development: Birth to 15 months

The moment your baby is born, his personality and emotions start to show through. He cries when he is unhappy, he's bright eyed when he's enjoying himself, and he looks around the room when he is bored. You'll discover more and more of your baby's characteristics over the next 15 months as you play with him, stimulate him, and try to settle him into a stable feeding and sleeping routine. His basic human need to mix with other people emerges during these first months as well, as he begins to become aware of other people and starts to seek attention from them.

Emotional Types

Every baby is different, with his own special and unique set of personal traits. However, psychologists have identified three main types of temperament in young children.

First, there is the easy child who copes happily with new experiences. He plays enthusiastically with new toys, sleeps and eats regularly, and adjusts easily to change. In contrast, the difficult child is the exact opposite. He resists any routine, cries a lot, takes a long time to finish his meals, and sleeps fitfully. And then there is the slow-to-warm-up child who is rather easy-going and passive. He doesn't get actively involved in anything and waits for the world to come to him. You can probably see aspects of all these types in your baby!

Nobody knows for sure where these emotional characteristics come from. Almost certainly, though, his personality and ability to relate to

Right: Your baby forms a close emotional bond with you.

others is a combination of the characteristics he was born with and the way you raise him during childhood. There is also some evidence that emotional development begins during pregnancy. For example, studies have found that when a pregnant woman is angry, afraid, or anxious, her emotional condition releases certain chemicals and hormones into her bloodstream that can affect the fetus, making the unborn baby restless and active.

Forming an Attachment

The biggest influence on your growing baby's social and emotional development during this early phase of his life, however, is bonding – that is, the two-way emotional attachment that he forms with you. This special relationship between you and your baby has a huge influence on his personality, emotional stability, and friendliness.

Fortunately, your baby has an innate ability to form a close relationship with you. For instance, his hearing is tuned to pick up the sound of your voice, his vision enables him to focus clearly on your face during feeding, he can use his cries to express his feelings to you, and he is even more responsive to the smell of your breast milk than he is to the breast milk of a stranger. These inborn social skills mean that bonding is a natural process, one that both you and your baby are ready for.

Here are some facts about bonding:
• **it doesn't have to happen at birth.** Although some moms and dads claim to love their baby the

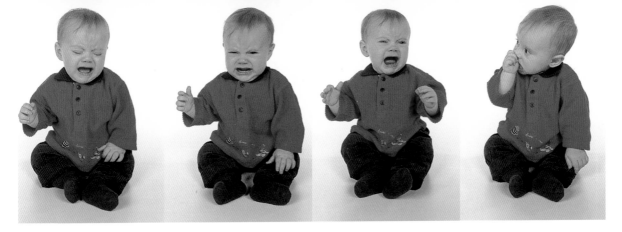

second they set eyes on him, most parents take much longer to feel their baby is really theirs. At least 40 percent of perfectly normal mothers take more than a week – and sometimes months – to bond with their baby. So there is no reason to worry if it was not love at first sight for you.

• **it doesn't have to be all-or-nothing.** For most parents and babies, bonding is a gradual process. Like all your other relationships, the connection formed with your baby needs time. It is not a case that you have no bond with him one day and then suddenly the next day you have. The emotional attachment typically builds up day by day, month by month.

• **it doesn't happen with only one parent.** There is plenty of evidence that your baby is capable of forming an emotional attachment with more than one person at a time. He can have a psychological bond with you, and also with your partner, and with his grandparents. Each of these different relationships is very special to him, and each contributes in its own way to his social and emotional development.

Get Involved

A strong connection between you and your baby brings him a sense of well-being, makes him feel safe and secure, provides a solid foundation for him to build future social relationships with others, and helps him learn to trust other people. And bonding is great for you, too, because it makes you feel good about yourself as a parent. It's a wonderful thought to know that your baby loves you and feels safe with you.

There's lots you can do to help this all-important psychological process along the way. Most importantly, try to relax when you are with your baby so that you can each enjoy the other's company. Of course, caring for him is demanding and you probably feel that you never have a minute to yourself; you may even have doubts about your own skills as a parent. Bear in mind, though, that your baby will be more comfortable with you when he senses you are at ease with him.

Physical love plays a large part in his social and emotional development, too. He just

Right: A close bond will enable you to understand and respond to your baby's needs more easily.

Above: At 6 months some babies have developed the habit of thumb sucking, which can act as a ready comforter in moments of distress.

adores a cuddle from you, or from any other familiar person. There is something very special about being held firmly and gently in the arms of a loving adult. The closeness, the warmth, the body contact that are all part of a caring cuddle greatly increase his contentment and confidence.

Social and Emotional Development

Age	Skill
1 week	She likes you to be with her as much as possible, and when your face is close enough to her, she stops what she is doing long enough to stare at you.
1 month	Feeding becomes not just a source of physical nourishment but also an opportunity for contentment and closeness with you.
2 months	By this time you have seen her first smile, a clear demonstration of her ability to have fun and to take pleasure from social contact.
3 months	Your baby is a lot more responsive to any adult who shows interest in her, and her need for human attention is now obvious.
4 months	Your baby uses nonverbal communication in order to draw you – or any other familiar adult – into spending time with her.
5 months	She has formed an attachment to her favorite cuddly toy and likes to have this object close to her when she is going to sleep.
6 months	At around this time she probably shows the first signs of shyness and social anxiety when she realizes that she is in the presence of an unfamiliar adult.
7 months	Your 7-month-old child has no difficulty in accurately conveying her negative feelings as well as her positive emotions to you.

From Birth to 7 Months

What to Do

Support your baby's head with one hand and her back and shoulders with the other, so that she faces you. Then gradually bring her face within 6–9 inches of yours. As she starts to recognize you, her body will move with excitement.

While feeding your baby, gently talk to her. Her attention will immediately turn to you, and she will make eye contact with you. She will continue to look at you even if she pauses for a few moments during her feeding.

The way to make your baby smile – and this typically begins when she is around 6 weeks old – depends on your baby's individual personality. However, if you beam at her brightly, chances are that her face will break into a huge grin, too.

You'll notice that she often cries when left alone yet stops the moment you come over to see what's the matter. Suddenly she changes from tears to smiles, from sadness to pleasure, as her social and emotional need is met by your company.

Watch your child closely when playing with her. Her excited body language and delighted facial expressions serve two social purposes: they tell you that she is pleased, and they act as encouragement for you to continue playing with her.

Your child probably has a particular cuddly toy – or maybe even her crib blanket – that she prefers to hold when nodding off to sleep. She snuggles up against this item because it gives her comfort and makes her feel emotionally secure.

If you are with your infant, say, shopping together in the supermarket, and a total stranger comes over to speak to her, you may find that she leans toward you and bursts out crying. Even if she holds back her tears, she seeks your protection.

Try taking a toy away from her while she plays with it. Her initial reaction will be to resist, perhaps by gripping onto it. If you do succeed in removing the toy from her, she will be furious with you and make an enormous fuss.

Social and Emotional Development

Age	Skill
8 months	Her improved self-confidence and social awareness allows her to initiate social contact with other adults, even if she doesn't know them particularly well.
9 months	She becomes curious about other babies her own age, even though she can't talk to them or even play with them.
10 months	Your growing infant is more aware of the emotional significance of cuddles and hugs, now that she can give them as well as receive them.
11 months	Whenever her wishes are blocked, her threshold for frustration is quickly crossed and she loses her temper quite easily.
1 year	She loves playing any game or taking part in any activity that involves social interaction between you and her. The social connection matters more than the activity itself.
13 months	Although she still relies totally on you for all her daily needs, your child's innate desire to become independent shows through in small ways.
14 months	Your child's confidence has grown, but she may be afraid of strangers even though you are beside her.
15 months	Her determination shows through as she tries to stamp her authority over you. Tantrums are common with children of this age when they can't get their own way.

From 8 to 15 Months

What to Do

Have a chat with a friend in your child's presence. She might try to grab your attention by passing either you or your friend one of her toys. That's her way of saying, "I would like us to play with each other" and she expects you to join in.

If possible, sit your child beside another baby around the same age. She will stare with complete fascination at this other child, and may reach out to touch, poke, or pull at her until the focus of her interest complains about this unwanted attention.

Cuddle her. Her improved hand and arm control, coupled with her increased understanding of the effect she has on you, means that she now reciprocates the loving reaction – hugs are two-way, and she is no longer just a passive recipient.

You need to watch your infant's reactions very closely when she plays with a puzzle toy or when you tell her that she isn't allowed to do something. The transformation from a settled child into an outraged infant takes only a second at this age.

Action rhymes, such as "Round and Round the Garden" and "This Little Piggy," make her giggle with delight. Likewise, she enjoys "peek-a-boo" and "Pat-a-Cake" games, which require close social contact between the two of you.

When dressing or changing your toddler, let her play her part if she wants. For instance, if she puts her hands out as you bring a pullover toward her, give her a big hug so that she knows you are pleased. Do this each time she tries to help in this way.

Take her to a parent-and-toddler group so that she has the opportunity to mix with other children. But stay with her. She may be perfectly happy until a child approaches her – and at that point she'll probably be filled with terror and try to hide behind you.

You need to be very calm and patient with your child when it comes to setting limits. The moment she grasps that you have said "no" to her and that you mean it, she will explode with rage in the hope of forcing you to change your mind.

Stimulating Social and Emotional Development: Birth to 3 Months

During these first few months, you and your baby need time to get to know each other. You gradually learn the meaning of his cries, facial expressions, and body movements, and he steadily learns the meaning of your voice tones, manner, and touch. The key to his satisfactory early emotional and social development is establishing a loving relationship with you.

BOTTLE-FEEDING OR BREAST-FEEDING

Whereas scientific evidence proves that breast-feeding wins hands down when it comes to protecting your baby from infections during this early period, not one research study suggests either bottle-feeding or breast-feeding has any particular benefit in helping you and your baby form a bond.

The style of feeding does have an effect, however. For instance, if you are tense and hurried when feeding him (whether using breast or bottle), he'll be tense, too; if you are irritable with him, he will sense this and have difficulty feeding. In other words, try to think positively during feeding.

Suitable Suggestions

The best help you can give your baby is to relax when you are with him. That's easier said than done, of course, because the stresses and strains of keeping up with his constant feeding, changing, and bathing needs can seem overwhelming at times. And if things don't go entirely as planned because, for instance, he doesn't take his bottle properly or because he cries for no apparent reason, you are likely to become anxious. Yet if you are tense and strained with your baby, he'll soon feel like that, too. So it's worth making a special effort to be at ease in his company.

Another way to help you and your baby forge a strong emotional connection is to soothe him when he appears distressed. Your baby cries for any one of a large number of reasons, ranging from hunger to pain, from loneliness to tiredness, and it's hard for you to know the real explanation for his upset. The problem is that he can't speak to you to say what troubles him. But you can try to soothe him anyway.

You'll develop a repertoire of strategies for stopping his tears, including cuddling him, swaddling him, playing soft music to him, taking him for a ride in the car, and playing with him. The success of these different techniques will vary from week to week, depending on his mood, but the main thing is that you make a good attempt at finding a way to calm your baby.

Below: Close physical contact is reassuring to a new baby.

Above: Kissing, cuddling, and talking to your new baby will help you learn to handle her in a calm and relaxed way.

You can also help his social development by letting him be held by other adults. True, he quickly gets used to your handling, warmth, and smell, and he likes that. However, there is no harm in letting other caring relatives and friends give him a cuddle when they visit. This won't at all threaten the integrity of your emotional attachment with him, and it will strengthen his sociability. He'll enjoy a cuddle from his grandmother or from your best pal, even though he prefers you to hold him. This gets him used to being with other people from an early age, laying the foundation for future social relationships.

Below: If you enjoy it, feeding your baby can be a time when you feel very close to him.

✦✦✦✦✦✦✦ Top·Tips ✦✦✦✦✦✦✦

1. Have confidence in yourself as a parent. Tell yourself that you will be a great parent. Act confidently and calmly when managing your new baby. Your self-belief will steadily increase as your experience grows.

2. Make lots of eye contact with your young baby. He loves it when you look deep into his eyes, because attention builds his confidence. It also teaches him the essential social skill of looking other people in the eyes when talking to them.

3. Let him know that you are interested in him. He needs to feel that he matters to you, and the best way of demonstrating this is by giving him lots of attention, by talking lovingly to him, and by smiling at him and giving him lots of cuddles.

4. Try to develop a stable feeding and sleeping routine. His nutritional and sleep needs change quickly during this period, and routines can be very difficult to establish. However, most babies are more settled in a steady routine.

5. Take him with you when you go out. It's good for him to see a range of faces and hear different voices, whether at the supermarket or in the street. This heightens his interest in other people and builds his social confidence.

Q If I go to my baby every time he cries, am I encouraging him to be attention-seeking?

A A baby left unattended while crying may feel lonely, isolated, and insecure. After all, crying is your baby's main way of communicating with you. When he is a bit older, you might decide to wait a moment before responding, but at this young age he cries because he needs you.

Q By what age should my baby have formed an emotional bond with me?

A That depends entirely on you and your baby. There is no "typical" time span. However, psychological research has found that a child who has not formed a secure psychological connection with a caring adult by the time he is around the age of 4 years is likely to have social difficulties throughout his life.

 **Toys:** cuddly crib toy, rattles, gentle music box to play while feeding or cuddling him, floor multi-gym

Stimulating Social and Emotional Development: 4 to 6 Months

Your infant's social skills increase as her need to mix with others intensifies. She starts to become more aware of other people around her and uses nonverbal communication to interact with them; she thrives on attention. But despite this enthusiasm to have company, her social confidence remains very fragile – the moment she sets eyes on a stranger she may well burst into tears.

ENDURING TRAITS

Babies vary greatly in their sensitivity and moods. Maybe your baby is one of those who is very dramatic when it comes to expressing her emotions; perhaps she howls loudly the minute anything goes wrong and whines and moans most of the time. Or maybe she is an even-tempered infant who happily goes with the flow and deals calmly with life's little challenges.

Whatever your baby's particular emotional characteristics, you will find that you adjust to them. Results from psychological research suggest that many of these important personality traits that are present during the early months are usually stable, in that they tend to stick with the baby for the rest of her life.

Suitable Suggestions

Respond eagerly when your baby communicates. Should she smile at you or make sounds to grab your attention, go over to her and play with her. Reciprocate her gestures, so that if she smiles, you smile back, if she passes you a toy, you pass her a toy, and so on. This reinforces her social skills. There will be times when she is happy to play on her own, especially as she nears the 6-month point, but for the time being she likes to have your attention whenever possible.

This doesn't mean, though, that you should be there with her for every second of the day. Part of social and emotional development involves your child establishing an element of independence, of managing on her own without you right beside her all the time. If you rush over to her whenever she calls for you out of boredom, your baby between the ages of 4 and 6 months will never learn how to amuse herself. During this period of her life, try to make sure there are times when she

Right: At around 6 months babies can begin to grasp basic reciprocal communication.

is left to play in the crib on her own. This strengthens her self-sufficiency.

Her innate desire to explore, coupled with her increased hand–eye coordination and movement skills, results in a whole new range of discovery opportunities opening up for her. The downside of this is that she might get herself into situations that prove difficult or frightening for her – for instance, when she crawls behind the sofa and ends up jammed against the wall,

Above: At this age babies will show interest in other babies, though this is usually short-lived.

Q Should I play with my 5-month-old when she wakes during the night?

A Of course you need to comfort her. Yet there is a danger that if you turn night-waking into an enjoyable play episode, you may actually encourage her to wake up more frequently. A more effective strategy is to settle her, reassure her, and then let her go back to sleep.

Q Is it true that as babies, boys tend to be more difficult to manage than girls?

A There is not a great deal of research evidence to support this idea. However, it is generally true that baby boys tend to be more adventurous than baby girls, but this could be because parents let boys behave this way, whereas they discourage their girls from displaying such high-spirited behavior.

Toys: child-safe mirror with handles, small plastic blocks with a container, plastic or cloth books, small soft ball

✦✦✦✦✦✦✦ Top·Tips ✦✦✦✦✦✦✦

1. Let her play alongside other children her age. Although she will not play with them and might even just sit and stare at them, these other children will be of great interest to her. She watches and learns from their actions.

2. Talk to other people when she is with you. Your young baby needs to learn that language is a key part of most social interactions. Seeing you chat with people whom you meet provides a good model for her to copy.

3. Reassure her when she is shy with an unfamiliar adult. When she hides because a stranger talks to her, hold her hand, cuddle her, and tell her not to be afraid. Your reassurance helps her overcome this dip in her confidence.

4. React to her sense of humor. The ability to laugh is an effective social skill. So laugh heartily when you hear her laugh, and try to make her smile when she has a serious expression on her face.

5. Don't pander to her grumpy moments. If your child is irritable at times, keep talking to her and playing with her anyway. If you simply leave her alone when she is moody, her irritability will probably last longer.

or when she reaches for an object the table and succeeds in bringing it crashing down on her head. Your child can be unnerved by these events, and might become timid and apprehensive.

Boost her confidence when you see this happening. Comfort her, calm her, wipe away her tears, and then encourage her to start exploring again. The great thing about your baby is that she will soon forget a bad experience if you are there to cheer her up. If her self-belief suffers a setback, help her regain her confidence through your support and encouragement.

Below: A 4-month-old baby is very dependent on you for his entertainment and will probably play alone only for short periods.

Stimulating Social and Emotional Development: 7 to 9 Months

Your infant is less passive in the company of others. Now he is more outgoing socially and makes active attempts to respond to other people. Although he hasn't any meaningful speech yet, he will babble loudly when someone talks to him – this is his form of sociable conversation. He has no difficulty letting you know when he is in a bad mood!

COMFORTERS

Most infants become fond of a cuddly toy and like to have it with them. If yours has a comforter (so-called because the object makes him feel contented), he adores the cuddly toy even though it is dirty, ragged, and might even have bits missing. He loves the familiar feel and smell of the object.

Using a comforter does not mean your child is afraid or timid. In fact, there is no link between comforters in early childhood and emotional instability later on; if anything, evidence from studies shows that infants who become attached to a comforter are often more confident when they start attending school.

Suitable Suggestions

Increase your expectations of your baby's sociability. Whereas when he was younger you might have chatted to him without expecting any reasonable response, it's time for you to give him an opportunity to react. So when you talk to him, leave a pause for him to babble back at you; when you ask him a question such as "Do you want another drink?" look for an answer in his facial expression, body movements, and sounds instead of just giving him the drink anyway. Your encouragement will make him realize that he needs to get involved.

By now you should have begun to have clear ideas on discipline for use with your infant. Remember that discipline is not about controlling your child, but about encouraging his awareness of others and his understanding that other people have feelings just like him. Rules about behavior enhance his social awareness and help him establish self-control. Yet this doesn't mean he will happily do as you ask!

He knows the full meaning of the word "no" and may be absolutely furious with you when

Below: By 8 and 6 months these two babies are curious about each other and will interact.

Left: By 8 months babies enjoy their routine and will get excited when they know something they like is about to happen – such as the daily bath.

you stand in his way. That's a normal, healthy emotional reaction. However, you can help him gain control over his temper at this age by calming him and by standing

your ground. Don't give in to his angry demands. Through this process, he learns how to modify his own behavior and to develop sensitivity toward others.

A stable daily routine is helpful for your child's emotional development at this age. Meals at regular times and a reasonably fixed time for bed each night enable him to structure his day, and this structure contributes to his overall sense of security and well-being.

You'll find that he enjoys the familiarity of, for instance, his prebath and prebedtime routine because these actions signal what is about to come. He'll start to smile when he sees you bring his own bath towel from the cupboard or when he catches sight of you tidying his crib toys. Structure makes him feel safe. Of course you need to be flexible; in general, though, routine is emotionally beneficial for your child.

Below: At this age a baby still needs frequent reassurance and usually likes to know that you are near at hand.

✦✦✦✦✦✦✦ Top·Tips ✦✦✦✦✦✦✦

1. Continue to show your child that you love him. Regular demonstrations that you love and value him increase his self-confidence. He soaks up every drop of parental love you put his way and responds by acting lovingly toward you.

2. Make sure he achieves success in things he does. Success increases his "feel-good" factor and confidence. For instance, completing a puzzle toy or managing to bring a spoon to his mouth by himself has a very positive effect on him.

3. Take him along to a parent-and-toddler group. He's still not ready to play cooperatively with other children (and won't be for a long time) but that doesn't stop him from enjoying being in their presence. This experience stimulates his social enthusiasm.

4. Give him plenty of praise. Your verbal praise and approval matters very much to your baby aged between 7 and 9 months. It acts as encouragement to persevere while also boosting his self-esteem.

5. Use a baby-sitter so that you can go out without him. Aside from the benefits to you of going out on your own, it's good for your baby to get used to someone else's care. He'll quickly adapt to this temporary arrangement.

Q My baby is 8 months old but still cries extremely easily. How can I make him more robust?

A He probably cries so much because this is an effective way of getting your attention. Start to ignore some of his crying episodes unless you are sure there is something seriously wrong. His tears may flow less frequently when he realizes they don't achieve the desired effect.

Q Should I let my 9-month-old baby continue to suck a pacifier?

A It's entirely up to you. The biggest hazard facing a child who sucks a pacifier at this age is that of poor hygiene. He probably throws it on the ground, picks it up, and puts it straight into his mouth, which makes him vulnerable to germs. So you should do your best to keep his pacifier clean.

Toys: carriage rattle, plastic grab-ring, cuddly small animal, teething ring, jack-in-the-box toy, single-picture cardboard book

Stimulating Social and Emotional Development: 10 to 12 Months

Your child's main emotional characteristics are clear and strong, and you can probably now predict how she will behave in most situations. However, her increased awareness of the world around her causes a temporary halt to the growth in her sociability; her attachment to you becomes more intense, and her desire to mix with others slows down a little at this stage.

THE AMBITIOUS TODDLER

Despite her clinging behavior and fear of strangers, your toddler is very ambitious and has a tremendous belief in her own abilities. No challenge is too great for her once she has made up her mind to achieve it.

In reality, however, her ambitions outstrip her ability, and this means you may find a sharp increase in episodes of tearfulness and frustration. For instance, she is extremely unhappy when the cushions of the sofa are impossibly high for her to reach, or when the door handle is too high for her to turn. She needs you to comfort her when these desired goals elude her.

Suitable Suggestions

The typical toddler feels very secure with her parents and has an increased awareness of strangers. The ironic effect of these two trends is that you might find your child happy to play with you but more anxious with unfamiliar people, even though recently she was more socially adventurous. Don't be irritable with her when she clings tightly to you – this apparent increase in her emotional dependency on you will pass in a few months. She needs your patience and support at this time.

In the meantime, continue to encourage her to play in the presence of other children and continue to use other caregivers (for example a baby-sitter) when required. But do expect her to be

Right: Approaching a year, it is easier for your baby to begin to share games and activities with other members of the family.

a bit more clingy to you at this time. If she cries when you leave her with the baby-sitter – whereas before she didn't bother at all – give her lots of reassurance and then go out anyway. You can always call the baby-sitter a few minutes later to make sure she has settled.

You'll find that when you take your 1-year-old to parent-and-toddler group, there may be times when she crawls over to another child and snatches a toy from her hands. Your toddler doesn't do this out of malice; it's just

Left: Ironically, as your child becomes able to do more she may also become more clingy, as she identifies very strongly with her parents and is less accepting of strangers.

that she isn't mature enough to contemplate the emotional effect this has on the other child. And when her action causes the other child to burst out crying with shock, she stares with curiosity, unable to see the connection between her taking the toy and the other child's tears.

Respond calmly but firmly in these situations. Remember that part of your child's social and emotional development involves her increasing sensitivity to the wishes and feelings of others; she slowly learns that she doesn't live in a social vacuum, that her behavior has an effect on those around her. So take the toy from her, telling her quietly but clearly that she shouldn't take things from another child like that, and return the toy to the original owner. Your toddler will howl in protest and may try to reverse your decision, but return the toy anyway.

Above: Start to encourage good social behavior. You can begin to explain things like taking turns in simple terms.

••••••• Top•Tips •••••••

1. Use a familiar routine when leaving her with another caregiver. When you go out without her, follow the same format of saying goodbye, kissing her, then waving goodbye to her. Encourage her to reciprocate these actions to you.

2. Model good behavior. You should avoid the trap of constantly correcting her when she misbehaves. She is more likely to learn appropriate behavior if you tell her what she should do, instead of reprimanding her for what she shouldn't do.

3. Have fun with her. Toddlers can be very demanding to be with all day. But her confidence and social skills will improve when she knows that you are relaxed, laughing, and smiling in her company. Her sense of security increases as a result.

4. Take pride in her achievements. Your child needs constant encouragement to progress, but you need to ensure that she knows you are pleased with her progress so far. Praise her current achievements before going on to the next stage.

5. Give her social reassurance. Reassure your socially anxious infant by speaking words of support to her, by hugging her when necessary, by giving her lots of opportunities to be with others, and by praising her when she copes without tears.

Q Should I let my child hold the spoon at meals? She makes such a mess.

A She makes a mess because she can't do the job properly, but the only way she can learn is through practice. Try not to dampen her desire for independence, even though you could complete feeding more quickly on your own. Let her hold the spoon at least part of the time.

Q My 11-month-old baby cries whenever I leave her with someone else. Would it be better for me to sneak out of the house quietly when she isn't looking?

A This may work at first, but your infant will quickly learn your strategy and become very anxious even when you have no intention of sneaking out. It's better for you to tell her goodbye, cuddle her, reassure her, and then just go.

Toys: music box, cassettes with songs, plastic building blocks, floating bath toys, pop-up toy, nonglass child-safe mirror

Stimulating Social and Emotional Development: 13 to 15 Months

Your toddler can be more difficult to manage during this start to his second year. He wants to do more on his own and is not at all pleased if you set limits on his behavior. Tantrums may be frequent when he can't get his own way. He is curious about other people, and will stare uninhibitedly at anyone who attracts his attention.

FEARS

Toddlers this age are notoriously challenging and determined and can be remarkably confident with others. And yet this is also the time when small fears can develop. In fact, research confirms that most children have a least one fear from the age of 12 months onward, such as a fear of cats, dogs, insects, or wasps.

If your child does show fear of something, don't make a fuss, because that will intensify his terror. Instead, remain calm, reassure him that he will be fine, and just carry on with his normal routine. He will take his emotional lead from you – your relaxed, stable attitude will help him beat his fear.

Suitable Suggestions

Take your child with you outside when at all possible. People fascinate him and he loves watching them. If someone arouses his curiosity, he might toddle over to them and stick his face as close to theirs as he can; he is as likely to do this in the supermarket as he is at parent-and-toddler group. Bring him back to your side on these occasions and tell him not to stare (even though he doesn't fully understand what you mean). He'll gradually learn that such social closeness is not welcome.

Right: Your child will now positively relish attention from other people she knows well, such as grandparents.

Your 1-year-old has an increased sense of self, an increased awareness that he is an individual with his own likes and dislikes, his own strengths and weaknesses. This is a key part of his emotional development.

One easy technique – used by psychologists to test the development of a child's self-image – is to let your toddler play with a mirror. When you are sure he has studied his own reflection in it, distract his attention with another activity for a few seconds.

Left: Children of this age need plenty of physical outlets for their energies and find it great fun if you join in sometimes.

As you do this, discreetly put a red mark on his forehead (say, with lipstick) but without making him aware that you have done it. Then get him involved in looking at the mirror once again.

If his self-image is sufficiently mature, he will touch his forehead in the approximate

Left: Make some basic decisions about what behavior you will and will not tolerate and be consistent.

area of the red mark because he knows that this is his reflection and that therefore he must have that mark on his head. Approximately half of all children around the age of 15 months will try to touch the mark, compared with three quarters of all 2-year-olds and virtually all 3-year-olds.

You can encourage your toddler's sense of self by making a special point of using his name when you talk to him. He knows that this word is just for him and that when you look at him and say his name, you are referring to him alone. You can also help by starting to teach him the names of his body parts, such as hands, feet, eyes, ears, and so on. He's much too young to say these words, but he can start to understand them.

Below: Be prepared for tantrums when your child cannot get his own way, and accept that they are part and parcel of his becoming an individual.

✦✦✦✦✦✦ Top·Tips ✦✦✦✦✦✦

1. Give him advice on social skills. He needs you to point out to him, for instance, that he should pass the ball to the other child, and that he should say "hello" when he meets another person. He learns these social skills gradually.

2. Praise appropriate social behavior. When your child acts positively in a social setting (for instance, if he shares his toys or smiles at another child) give him a cuddle to show him that you are delighted with his behavior.

3. Don't pander to his fears. Your growing child won't learn to overcome a fear if you allow him to avoid the thing that frightens him. Keep to his normal daily routine despite his fear, rather than organizing his life around it.

4. Tackle jealousy when it arises. He may be resentful when you give attention to another toddler. This jealousy arises because he doesn't like sharing you. Talk to him until he calms down, then continue talking to his friend.

5. Have your evening meal with him occasionally. Try to include your toddler at times when having the evening meal with the rest of your family. He loves the social nature of a family meal.

Q&A

Q My toddler screams the place down if I put the light out before he is asleep. What should I do?

A Fit a dimmer switch to his light. Without saying anything, each night gradually set the light a bit dimmer than it was the night before. You'll find that after a period of perhaps three or four weeks, he can sleep without any night-light at all.

Q Our 14-month-old has insisted recently that he play only with me, not my partner. Is that normal?

A Phases of attachment to one parent in particular happen occasionally, but are temporary. Arrange for your partner to play with your toddler, to bathe him, feed him, and so on, even though he prefers your company. This will help the attachment to both of you remain strong.

Toys: plastic book with pictures, puzzle boards, pull-along toy, child-safe mirror, crayon and paper, plastic construction blocks

Index of Age Groups

1st week
emotional development
39
hand–eye coordination
38, 70–1, 74–5
language 39, 88–9
learning 39
movement 38, 52–3,
56–7
social development 39

1st month
emotional development
39, 124–5, 128–9
hand–eye coordination
38, 70–1, 74–5
language 38–9, 88–9,
92–3
learning 39, 106–7,
110–11
movement 38, 52–3,
56–7
social development 39,
124–5, 128–9

2nd month
emotional development
39, 124–5, 128–9
hand–eye coordination
38, 70–1, 74–5
language 38–9, 88–9,
92–3
learning 39, 106–7,
110–11
movement 38, 52–3,
56–7
social development 39,
124–5, 128–9

3rd month
emotional development
39, 124–5, 128–9

hand–eye coordination
38, 70–1, 74–5
language 38–9, 88–9,
92–3
learning 39, 106–7,
110–11
movement 38, 52–3,
56–7
social development 39,
124–5, 128–9

4th month
emotional development
41, 124–5, 130–31
hand–eye coordination
41, 70–1, 76–7
language 41, 88–9, 94–5
learning 41, 106–7,
112–13
movement 40, 52–3,
58–9
social development 41,
124–5, 130–1

5th month
emotional development
41, 124–5, 130–1
hand–eye coordination
40, 70–1, 76–7
language 41, 88–9, 94–5
learning 41, 106–7,
112–13
movement 40, 52–3,
58–9
social development 41,
124–5, 130–1

6th month
emotional development
41, 124–5, 130–1
hand–eye coordination
40, 70–1, 76–7

language 40, 88–9, 94–5
learning 41, 106–7,
112–13
movement 40, 52–3,
58–9
social development 41,
124–5, 130–1

7th month
emotional development
43, 124–5, 132–3
hand–eye coordination
42, 70–1, 78–9
language 43, 88–9, 96–7
learning 43, 106–7,
114–15
movement 42, 52–3,
60–1
social development 43,
124–5, 132–3

8th month
emotional development
43, 126–7, 132–3
hand–eye coordination
42–3, 72–3, 78–9
language 43, 90–1, 96–7
learning 43, 108–9,
114–15
movement 42, 54–5,
60–1
social development 43,
126–7, 132–3

9th month
emotional development
43, 126–7, 132–3
hand–eye coordination
42–3, 72–3, 78–9
language 43, 90–1, 96–7
learning 43, 108–9,
114–15

movement 42, 54–5,
60–1
social development 43,
126–7, 132–3

10th month
emotional development
45, 126–7, 134–5
hand–eye coordination
44, 72–3, 80–1
language 44, 90–1,
98–9
learning 45, 108–9,
116–17
movement 44, 54–5,
62–3
social development 45,
126–7, 134–5

11th month
emotional development
45, 126–7, 134–5
hand–eye coordination
44, 72–3, 80–1
language 44, 90–1, 98–9
learning 45, 108–9,
116–17
movement 44, 54–5,
62–3
social development 45,
126–7, 134–5

12th month
emotional development
45, 126–7, 134–5
hand–eye coordination
44, 72–3, 80–1
language 45, 90–1, 98–9
learning 45, 108–9,
116–17
movement 44, 54–5,
62–3

social development 45,
126–7, 134–5

13th month
emotional development
47, 126–7, 136–7
hand–eye coordination
46–7, 72–3, 82–3
language 47, 90–1
learning 47, 108–9,
118–19

movement 46, 54–5,
64–5
social development 47,
126–7, 136–7

14th month
emotional development
47, 126–7,
136–7
hand–eye coordination
46, 72–3, 82–3

language 47, 90–1
learning 47, 108–9,
118–19
movement 46, 54–5,
64–5
social development 47,
126–7, 136–7

15th month
emotional development
47, 126–7, 136–7

hand–eye coordination
47, 72–3, 82–3
language 47, 90–1
learning 47, 108–9,
118–19
movement 46, 54–5,
64–5
social development 47,
126–7, 136–7

General Index

A
achievements 17, 35,
113, 135
special needs 37
acquired learning skills
105
action-reaction 9, 78–9
action without
understanding 69
active learning 7, 104–5
activities, appropriate 7
activity, lack of 61
activity centers 112
adopted children 15
adults, other 129
advice 9
from grandparents 23
affection *see* love
age gap 19
agitation 57
amusement, to soothe
26
anger
baby's 79, 115
parent's 69
appearance, baby's 10
arm and hand
movements 24

attachment, emotional
see bonding
attention
baby wants 26
crying 27
parent to baby 7, 111,
129
attitude, parent to baby
10–11
authoritarian discipline
style 33
authoritarian
grandparents 23

B
babbling 86–7, 96, 97,
100
baby gyms 75
baby walker 61
baby words 96
baby-sitters 133
grandparents 23
balancing 58, 59, 60, 64
balls 83, 115
bare feet 65
bathing 59, 76–7
bedtime 31

learning 115
safety 81
bedrooms 31, 75
behavior
good 33, 135
social 137
biological differences 21
birth order 16–17
blinking 68
body language 24
parent's 25
body movements 24
bonding 122–3, 129
books
cloth 77
picture 74, 77, 97, 116
bottle-feeding 128
bottom-shuffling 51
boxes with lids 80
brain development 51
breast-feeding 128
bubbles, blowing 97

C
calmness
disciplining baby 33
frustrated baby 83

parent with baby
awake at night 31
parent with crying
baby 27
caregivers, other 134
cars, sleeping in 31
cause and effect 114
toys 113
chairs, climbing into 51,
65
challenges, breaking
down 35
characteristics, natural
17
child-proof home 62
children, company of
other 101
climbing, into chairs 51,
65
clinging 134
cloth books 77
clusters of gestures 25
cognition *see* learning
ability
color recognition 110
colors 101
come and get it games
114

comforters 132
commands, parent to
    baby 81
communication 23
    nonverbal 24–5
comparisons, siblings 19
concentration 112, 116
    limited 37
    weak 11
confidence
    baby's 34–5, 63
    in parenting ability 21,
        27, 111, 129
cooing 86
cooperation, siblings 19
crawling 50, 51, 60, 62,
    65, 114
cruising the furniture 62,
    63
crying 24, 26–7, 112,
    133, 135
    interpret to baby 93,
        94
    meanings 93, 94, 129
cuddles 21, 24, 26, 34,
    35, 123
    from other adults 129
cups
    filling and emptying 79
    trainer 29
curiosity, lacks 37
curtains 75

D

demand, feeding on 28
democratic discipline
    style 33
development
    summary 14–47
    understanding 9
developmental checklists
    36
difficult children 122
directions, parent to
    baby 61

disagreements, siblings
    19
disappointment 35
discipline 32–3,
    132
    special needs 37
    styles 33
discussion, with others
    25
doctors 64
dressing and undressing
    83
drive, lack of 11

E

early speech 87
easy children 122
educational toys 113
efforts 17
emotional development
    122–37
    1st week 39
    1st to 3rd month 39,
        124–5, 128–9
    4th to 6th month 41,
        124–5, 130–1
    7th to 9th month 43,
        124–5, 132–3
    10th to 12th month 45,
        126–7, 134–5
    13th to 15th month 47,
        126–7, 136–7
    types 122, 130
emotional needs 9
encouragement
    complete task 78
    exploration 131
    good behavior 19, 33,
        135
    talking 101
    walking 34, 62, 64
    weaning 29
enthusiasm 77
environment, influence
    of 15

examples, setting good
    21
excitement, parent at
    new words 101
exploration 6, 69, 115
expression, lack of 11
expressive language 87
eye contact 7, 129

F

facial expressions 24
facing games 61
failure 35
falls 65
family meals 137
fear 130, 136, 137
    of new toys 83
feeding 28–9, 81, 115,
    135
    bottle 128
    breast 128
    himself 77, 80, 81
    on demand 28
    on schedule 28
    strategy 29
feet
    bare 65
    movements 24
finger food 77
finger puppets 101
firstborn children 16, 17,
    19, 116
first steps 50, 62
first word 87, 99, 100
food see feeding
frustration 35, 60, 82,
    83, 119, 134

G

games
    balls 83
    come and get it 114
    cups 79
    facing 61

hand 81
    kicking 65
    listening 93
    movement 58, 63
    musical instruments
        79
    peek-a-boo 96, 97
    pretend 100, 117,
        118
gender differences 20–1
    language 97
    social development
        131
gestures 101
    reciprocating 130
gives up easily 78
good behavior 135
grandparents 22–3, 136
grumpiness 131
guilt feelings, with
    crying baby 27

H

hand control, weak 37
hand–eye coordination
    8, 68–83
    1st week 38, 70–1,
        74–5
    1st to 3rd month 38,
        70–1, 74–5
    4th to 6th month 41,
        70–1, 76–7
    7th month 42–3, 70–1,
        78–9
    8th to 9th month 42–3,
        72–3, 78–9
    10th to 12th month 44,
        72–3, 80–1
    13th month 46–7,
        72–3, 82–3
    14th month 46, 72–3,
        82–3
    15th month 47, 72–3,
        82–3
hand games 81

hand movements,
    demonstrating 75
hand preferences 83
harness 65
head
    controlling 58
    supporting 57
health visitors 64
hearing 96
hearing discrimination
    105
help, with crying baby 27
heredity/environment
    debate see
    nature/nurture
    debate
holding, baby upright 57
holistic approach 8
hugs see cuddles
humor 131
hunger 29
hygiene, feeding 29

I

identification, special
    needs 36
imagination 118
imitation
    by baby 111
    of baby 25, 96
impulsive playing 119
independence 130
information, special
    needs 37
inherited learning skills
    105
inset-board puzzles 82
instructions, baby
    responds to 99
intelligence see learning
    ability
intelligence tests 117
interest, parent in baby's
    progress 17
irritability 11

J

jealousy 18, 137
jigsaws 119

K

kicking 57
    games 65
knowledge, of baby 9

L

language 8–9, 86–101
    1st week 39, 88–9
    1st to 3rd month 38–9,
        88–9, 92–3
    4th to 5th month 41,
        88–9, 94–5
    6th month 40, 88–9,
        94–5
    7th month 43, 88–9,
        96–7
    8th to 9th month 43,
        90–1, 96–7
    10th to 11th month
        44, 90–1, 98–9
    12th month 45, 90–1,
        98–9
    13th to 15th month
        47, 90–1, 100–1
    development 86–7
    gender differences 97
later-born children 17
laughing 7, 77, 131
learned differences,
    gender 21
learning 6, 9, 104–19
    1st week 39
    1st to 3rd month 39,
        106–7, 110–11
    4th to 6th month 41,
        106–7, 112–13
    7th to 9th month 43,
        106–7, 114–15
    10th to 12th month
        45, 108–9, 116–17

13th to 15th month
    47, 108–9, 118–19
    development 104–5
    learning ability 104
    learning skills see
        learning ability
legs 57
    movements 24
    raised 59
linguistic phrases 86
listening 87, 95
    games 93
    to children 17, 99
looking 68, 74
love 15, 21, 35, 123, 128,
    133
lying
    facedown 57, 59
    on back 56
    parent with baby 57

M

memory 115
middle children 16–17
milk 28, 29
mirrors 115
misery 57
misunderstandings,
    between parent and
    grandparent 23
mobiles, hanging 74, 111
modeling
    good behavior 135
    sounds 95
Moro reflex 69
mouth, exploring with 8,
    76, 82
movement 8, 50–65
    1st week 38, 52–3
    1st to 3rd month 38,
        52–3, 56–7
    4th to 6th month 40,
        52–3, 58–9
    7th month 42, 52–3,
        60–1

8th to 9th month 42,
    54–5, 60–1
    10th to 12th month
        44, 54–5, 62–3
    13th to 15th month
        46, 54–5, 64–5
    control 51
    development 51
    games 58, 63
    parent's 59
    rocking to soothe 26
music 95, 110
musical instruments 79

N

names
    baby's 95, 118, 137
    other people's 99
naming
    body parts 117, 119,
        137
    everyday objects 97,
        100
naps, timing 31
nature 14–15
nature/nurture debate
    14
nesting cubes 80
new baby, sibling rivalry
    19
night-light 137
no go areas 76
noise rhymes 97
noisy playing 79
nonverbal
    communication
    24–5, 86, 92
nourishment 29
nursery rhymes 98–9
nurture 14–15

O

object permanence 9
objects

naming everyday 97,
100
passing from hand to
hand 77
seeing small 115
within reach 7
only children 17
ornaments 76, 77
overstimulation 10, 11

P
pacifiers 98, 138
palmar grasp 68–9
parent-and-toddler
groups 133
parentese 92
partnership, stimulation 7
passing objects from
hand to hand 77
passivity 11, 80
patience, special needs
37
patterns, child-centered
75
peek-a-boo games 96, 97
permissive discipline
style 33
persistence
special needs 37
weaning 29
personality 16–17
physical contact 24
physical development,
slower 37
picture books 74, 77, 97,
116
picture cards 97
pincer grasp 78
playful grandparents 23
playing 104
encourage vocalization
93
extend 119
importance with
special needs 36

impulsive 119
noisy 79
parent with baby 111,
117
pretend 100, 117, 118
sand and water 119
siblings 19
sitting position 113
with grandparents 23
with household items
117
with other children
131
playpens 63
positive outlook, special
needs 37
positive reinforcement
33
practical actions 25
praise 133
effort 17
following rules 77
social behavior 137
walking 64
pregnancy 122
pretend play 100, 117,
118
pride 7
progress, little 63
punishment 32
physical 33
puzzles 82, 117

R
radio 113
reach, objects within 7
reach discrimination
104–5
reading stories 95, 99
reassurance 35
receptive language 87
reflexes 28, 68–9
blinking 68
Moro 69
palmar grasp 68–9

stepping 51
sucking 28, 68
swallowing 28
walking 57
relaxed attitude 123, 128
feeding 29
learning atmosphere
15
remote grandparents 23
repetition, talking 101
rolling 58, 59, 60
routines
actions 113, 117
daily 133
feeding 129
other caregivers 135
sleeping 31, 129
rules 32
explaining to baby 33
touching 76

S
safety
bathing 81
child-proof home 62
exploration 115
gates 62
hand–eye coordination
69
movement learning 61
observation 57
toddlers 64
touching 77
toys 75
sand and water play 119
schedule, feeding on 28
second children 16, 17
seeing, small objects 115
self-awareness, gender
issues 21
self-belief 34, 35, 63,
131
self-confidence 34
self-image 136–7
self-motivation 7

self-reflection 34–5
self-sufficiency 130
self-value 34
sex differences *see* gender
differences
shape recognition 110
shape-sorters 81, 83, 117
sharing, with
grandparents 23
shoes 65
shopping 64, 115
shyness 131
sibling rivalry 18–19
sidestepping 63
similarities, emphasize in
special needs 37
singing 93
sitting 58, 60, 77
special needs 37
skills, extending 7
sleeping 59
crying before 27
in cars 31
inability 11
patterns 30–1
waking at night 31,
131
slow-to-warm-up
children 122
smacking 33
small items 76
sociability 132
social confidence 129
social development
122–37
1st week 39
1st to 3rd month 39,
124–5, 128–9
4th to 6th month 41,
124–5, 130–1
7th month 43, 124–5,
132–3
8th to 9th month 43,
126–7, 132–3
10th to 12th month 45,
126–7, 134–5

13th to 15th month 47, 126–7, 136–7
social needs 9
social reassurance 135
social skills 137
solids, food 29
solutions, offering 81
songs 93, 98
soothing techniques 26, 128
sound groupings 98
sounds
  modeling 95
  to soothe 26
space, for exploration 65
speaking 87
special needs 36–7
speech, early 87
stacking rings 37, 78
stairs 65
standing position 61, 63
startle reflex see Moro reflex
stepping reflex 51
stereotypes
  gender 20
  grandparents 22
stimulation 10
  importance 7
  varied program 9
struggle 119
styles, grandparenting 22–3
success, enabling 63
sucking reflex 28, 68
support, for playing 81
swallowing reflex 28
swinging 63
symbolic thought 118

T
talking
  child to himself and toys 100, 101
  to baby 25, 35, 76, 92, 94–5, 99, 111
  to other people 131
tantrums 136, 137
taste discrimination 104
television 93, 99
temper 133
tension, between parent and grandparent 23
textures, varied 81
thinking skills see learning ability
thumb sucking 123
tickling 59, 61
tidying up 118–19
time
  completing tasks 83
  exploration 65
tiredness 11
  early parenthood 30
toddlers 19, 134
touch discrimination 104
touching 18, 68, 74
  rules 76
  soothing 26
towers 81, 82
toys
  birth to 3rd month 57, 74–5, 93, 110–11, 129
  4th to 6th month 59, 77, 95, 113, 131
  7th to 9th month 61, 97, 115, 133
  10th to 12th month 63, 80, 81, 99, 135
  13th to 15th month 65, 101, 119, 137
  age-appropriate 113
  cause and effect 113
  crib 56–7, 110–11
  dropping 61
  educational 113
  just out of reach 59
  musical instruments 99

new 83, 113
noisy 110
picking up 65
special 117
telephone 83
tying to carriage 113
wide range 21
traditional grandparents 23
trainer cups 29
tug-of-war 75
turn-taking 17
twins, studies of 15

U
uncomplaining baby 11
understimulation 10, 11
understand development 9
unsettled baby 11

V
video 97, 99
visual discrimination 104
vocabulary 87
vocalizations, parent reacts to baby's 93
voice, parent's 95

W
waking see sleeping
walking 50, 51, 63, 64
  late development 64
walking reflex 57
watching, parent of baby 25
water, pouring 81
weaning 28–9
welcome, for grandparents 23
words
  baby 96

first 87, 99, 100
parent's excitement at new 101

Y
youngest children 16, 17

Acknowledgments

Executive Editor – Jane McIntosh
Editor – Sharon Ashman
Executive Art Editor – Leigh Jones
Book Design – 2wo Design
Photography – Peter Pugh-Cook
Stylist – Aruna Mathur
Production Controller – Lucy Woodhead

The publisher would like to thank all the children and parents who took part in the photoshoot for this book for their time, energy, patience, and cooperation. We would also like to thank the following companies for allowing us to use their products:

All Seasons, 654–6 High Road, Tally Ho Corner, North Finchley, London N12 0NL

Benetton 0–12/Modus Publicity, 10–12 Heddon Street, London W1R 1DN

The Early Learning Centre, South Marston Park, Swindon, SN3 4TJ Tel: 01793 831300

Marks and Spencer Tel: 020 7268 3118

Simon Horn bed available through
Baby & Co, 12 Wetherby Gardens, London SW5 Tel: 020 7737 0574

First edition for the United States and Canada published by Barron's Educational Series, Inc., 2001.

First published 2001 in Great Britain under the title *Bright Baby* by Hamlyn, an imprint, part of Octopus Publishing Group Limited, 2–4 Heron Quays, Docklands, London E14 4JP, Great Britain

Copyright © 2001 by Octopus Publishing Group Limited

All inquiries should be addressed to:
Barron's Educational Series, Inc.
250 Wireless Boulevard
Hauppauge, New York 11788
http://www.barronseduc.com

International Standard Book No. 0-7641-1878-1
Library of Congress Catalog Card No. 00-110923
Printed in China
9 8 7 6 5 4 3 2